50 Joy of Cooking Recipes for Home

By: Kelly Johnson

Table of Contents

- Classic Spaghetti Carbonara
- Beef Stroganoff
- Chicken Tikka Masala
- Homemade Pizza
- Shrimp Scampi
- Vegetarian Chili
- French Onion Soup
- Pad Thai
- Beef Tacos
- Baked Salmon with Dill
- Greek Salad
- Mushroom Risotto
- Chicken Parmesan
- Beef and Broccoli Stir Fry
- Butternut Squash Soup
- Lasagna
- Teriyaki Chicken
- Ratatouille
- Pulled Pork Sandwiches
- Caesar Salad
- Beef Bourguignon
- Stuffed Bell Peppers
- Chicken Enchiladas
- Quiche Lorraine
- Thai Green Curry
- Eggplant Parmesan
- Paella
- Tandoori Chicken
- Corn Chowder
- Beef Wellington
- Baked Ziti
- Caprese Salad
- Chicken Satay
- Vegetarian Paella
- Clam Chowder
- Pork Schnitzel

- Gazpacho
- Chicken Marsala
- Spinach and Ricotta Stuffed Shells
- Tuna Nicoise Salad
- Bangers and Mash
- Lemon Garlic Roast Chicken
- Beef Kefta
- Egg Drop Soup
- Swedish Meatballs
- Pesto Pasta
- Chicken Caesar Wraps
- Moroccan Tagine
- Ratatouille
- Chocolate Lava Cakes

Classic Spaghetti Carbonara

Ingredients:

- Spaghetti pasta
- Guanciale (cured pork cheek) or pancetta (Italian bacon)
- Eggs
- Pecorino Romano cheese (or Parmesan)
- Black pepper

Instructions:

1. Cook spaghetti pasta in salted boiling water until al dente. Reserve some pasta water before draining.
2. While the pasta cooks, cut the guanciale or pancetta into small cubes or strips. Cook them in a skillet over medium heat until crispy.
3. In a bowl, whisk together eggs, grated Pecorino Romano cheese (or Parmesan), and black pepper.
4. Once the pasta is cooked, drain it and immediately add it to the skillet with the cooked guanciale or pancetta. Toss well to combine.
5. Remove the skillet from heat and quickly pour in the egg and cheese mixture, tossing the pasta continuously to coat it evenly. The heat from the pasta will cook the eggs gently, creating a creamy sauce.
6. If needed, add a splash of reserved pasta water to achieve a creamy consistency.
7. Serve immediately, garnished with additional grated cheese and black pepper if desired.

Enjoy your Classic Spaghetti Carbonara!

Beef Stroganoff

Ingredients:

- 1 lb (450g) beef sirloin or tenderloin, thinly sliced into strips
- 1 onion, finely chopped
- 2 cloves garlic, minced
- 8 oz (225g) mushrooms, sliced
- 1 tablespoon olive oil
- 2 tablespoons butter
- 1 tablespoon all-purpose flour
- 1 cup beef broth
- 1 tablespoon Dijon mustard
- 1/2 cup sour cream
- Salt and pepper, to taste
- Fresh parsley, chopped, for garnish
- Egg noodles or rice, for serving

Instructions:

1. Heat olive oil in a large skillet over medium-high heat. Add the beef strips and cook until browned on all sides. Remove beef from skillet and set aside.
2. In the same skillet, add butter and sauté the onion until softened and translucent, about 3-4 minutes. Add garlic and cook for another minute until fragrant.
3. Add the sliced mushrooms to the skillet and cook until they release their moisture and begin to brown, about 5-7 minutes.
4. Sprinkle flour over the mushroom mixture and stir well to coat. Cook for 1-2 minutes to cook out the raw flour taste.
5. Gradually add beef broth to the skillet, stirring constantly to prevent lumps. Bring to a simmer and cook until the sauce thickens, about 5-7 minutes.
6. Stir in Dijon mustard and season with salt and pepper to taste.
7. Return the cooked beef strips to the skillet and simmer for 2-3 minutes to heat through.
8. Remove the skillet from heat and stir in sour cream until well combined.
9. Serve Beef Stroganoff hot over egg noodles or rice, garnished with chopped parsley.

Enjoy your Beef Stroganoff! It's creamy, savory, and perfect for a cozy meal.

Chicken Tikka Masala

Ingredients:

For the marinade:

- 1 lb (450g) boneless, skinless chicken thighs or breasts, cut into bite-sized pieces
- 1/2 cup plain yogurt
- 1 tablespoon ginger-garlic paste (or finely minced ginger and garlic)
- 1 tablespoon lemon juice
- 1 teaspoon ground cumin
- 1 teaspoon ground coriander
- 1/2 teaspoon turmeric powder
- 1/2 teaspoon cayenne pepper (adjust to taste)
- 1/2 teaspoon paprika
- Salt and pepper, to taste

For the sauce:

- 2 tablespoons vegetable oil or ghee
- 1 onion, finely chopped
- 2 cloves garlic, minced
- 1-inch piece of ginger, grated
- 1 teaspoon ground cumin
- 1 teaspoon ground coriander
- 1 teaspoon paprika
- 1/2 teaspoon turmeric powder
- 1/2 teaspoon cayenne pepper (adjust to taste)
- 1 can (14 oz / 400g) crushed tomatoes
- 1 cup heavy cream or coconut milk
- Salt, to taste
- Fresh cilantro, chopped, for garnish

Instructions:

1. In a bowl, combine all the ingredients for the marinade. Add the chicken pieces and toss until well coated. Cover and refrigerate for at least 1 hour, or ideally overnight for best flavor.
2. Preheat the oven to 400°F (200°C). Arrange the marinated chicken pieces on a baking sheet lined with parchment paper. Bake for 15-20 minutes or until the chicken is cooked through and slightly charred around the edges. Alternatively, you can grill the chicken pieces until cooked.
3. In a large skillet or pot, heat vegetable oil or ghee over medium heat. Add chopped onion and sauté until softened and translucent, about 5-7 minutes.

4. Add minced garlic and grated ginger to the skillet. Sauté for another 1-2 minutes until fragrant.
5. Stir in ground cumin, ground coriander, paprika, turmeric powder, and cayenne pepper. Cook the spices for about 1 minute until fragrant.
6. Pour in crushed tomatoes and simmer for 10-15 minutes, stirring occasionally, until the sauce thickens and the flavors meld together.
7. Stir in heavy cream or coconut milk, and salt to taste. Simmer for another 5 minutes until the sauce is heated through.
8. Add the cooked chicken tikka pieces to the sauce. Simmer gently for a few minutes to allow the flavors to combine.
9. Garnish with chopped fresh cilantro before serving.

Serve Chicken Tikka Masala hot with steamed basmati rice or naan bread. Enjoy the creamy, aromatic flavors of this classic Indian dish!

Homemade Pizza

Ingredients:

For the pizza dough:

- 2 1/4 cups (280g) all-purpose flour
- 1 teaspoon sugar
- 1 teaspoon salt
- 1 tablespoon olive oil
- 3/4 cup (180ml) warm water
- 1 packet (2 1/4 teaspoons) active dry yeast

For the pizza toppings (you can customize these to your liking):

- 1/2 cup tomato sauce or pizza sauce
- 1 1/2 cups shredded mozzarella cheese
- Toppings such as pepperoni, sliced bell peppers, sliced onions, mushrooms, olives, etc.
- Fresh basil leaves (optional)
- Grated Parmesan cheese (optional)
- Crushed red pepper flakes (optional)

Instructions:

1. **Prepare the pizza dough:**
   - In a small bowl, combine warm water, sugar, and yeast. Let it sit for about 5-10 minutes until foamy.
   - In a large mixing bowl, combine flour and salt. Make a well in the center and add olive oil and the yeast mixture.
   - Stir together until a dough forms. Transfer the dough onto a lightly floured surface and knead for about 5-7 minutes until smooth and elastic.
   - Place the dough in a lightly oiled bowl, cover with a damp cloth or plastic wrap, and let it rise in a warm place for about 1-2 hours until doubled in size.
2. **Preheat the oven:**
   - Preheat your oven to the highest temperature it can go (typically around 500°F/260°C) and place a pizza stone or upside-down baking sheet inside to preheat as well.
3. **Shape the pizza:**
   - Once the dough has risen, punch it down and divide it into two equal portions for smaller pizzas or keep it whole for one larger pizza.
   - On a lightly floured surface, roll out the dough into a circle or rectangle of your desired thickness.
4. **Assemble the pizza:**
   - Transfer the rolled-out dough onto a piece of parchment paper (for easy transfer to the hot pizza stone or baking sheet).

- Spread tomato sauce or pizza sauce evenly over the dough, leaving a small border around the edges.
- Sprinkle shredded mozzarella cheese over the sauce.
- Add your desired toppings evenly over the cheese.
5. **Bake the pizza:**
    - Carefully transfer the assembled pizza (with the parchment paper) onto the preheated pizza stone or baking sheet in the oven.
    - Bake for 10-12 minutes, or until the crust is golden brown and the cheese is melted and bubbly.
6. **Finish and serve:**
    - Remove the pizza from the oven and let it cool slightly before slicing.
    - Garnish with fresh basil leaves, grated Parmesan cheese, and crushed red pepper flakes if desired.
    - Slice and serve hot. Enjoy your delicious homemade pizza!

Feel free to experiment with different toppings and flavors to create your favorite homemade pizza!

Shrimp Scampi

Ingredients:

- 1 lb (450g) large shrimp, peeled and deveined
- Salt and pepper, to taste
- 3 tablespoons unsalted butter
- 2 tablespoons olive oil
- 4 cloves garlic, minced
- 1/4 teaspoon red pepper flakes (optional)
- 1/2 cup dry white wine (such as Pinot Grigio or Sauvignon Blanc)
- Juice of 1 lemon
- Zest of 1 lemon
- 1/4 cup chopped fresh parsley
- Cooked pasta (linguine or spaghetti), for serving
- Freshly grated Parmesan cheese, for serving

Instructions:

1. **Prepare the shrimp:**
    - Pat the shrimp dry with paper towels and season with salt and pepper.
2. **Cook the shrimp:**
    - In a large skillet, heat 1 tablespoon of butter and 1 tablespoon of olive oil over medium-high heat.
    - Add the shrimp in a single layer and cook for 1-2 minutes per side until pink and cooked through. Do this in batches if necessary to avoid overcrowding the skillet. Transfer cooked shrimp to a plate and set aside.
3. **Make the sauce:**
    - In the same skillet, add the remaining 2 tablespoons of butter and 1 tablespoon of olive oil.
    - Add minced garlic and red pepper flakes (if using). Sauté for about 1 minute until garlic is fragrant.
4. **Deglaze the skillet:**
    - Pour in the white wine and bring to a simmer, scraping up any browned bits from the bottom of the skillet with a wooden spoon.
5. **Finish the sauce:**
    - Stir in lemon juice and lemon zest. Let the sauce simmer for 2-3 minutes until slightly reduced and flavors are melded together.
6. **Combine shrimp and sauce:**
    - Return the cooked shrimp to the skillet. Stir gently to coat the shrimp in the sauce. Cook for another minute until shrimp are heated through.
7. **Serve:**
    - Stir in chopped parsley.
    - Serve Shrimp Scampi hot over cooked pasta (linguine or spaghetti).
    - Garnish with freshly grated Parmesan cheese and additional parsley if desired.

Enjoy your homemade Shrimp Scampi with a side of crusty bread and a glass of white wine for a delightful meal!

Vegetarian Chili

Ingredients:

- 1 tablespoon olive oil
- 1 onion, chopped
- 3 cloves garlic, minced
- 1 bell pepper (any color), diced
- 2 carrots, diced
- 2 celery stalks, diced
- 1 zucchini, diced
- 1 tablespoon chili powder
- 1 teaspoon ground cumin
- 1 teaspoon smoked paprika
- 1/2 teaspoon dried oregano
- 1/4 teaspoon cayenne pepper (optional, for heat)
- Salt and pepper, to taste
- 1 can (14 oz / 400g) diced tomatoes
- 2 cans (15 oz each) beans (such as kidney beans, black beans, or pinto beans), drained and rinsed
- 1 cup corn kernels (fresh, canned, or frozen)
- 2 cups vegetable broth
- 1 tablespoon tomato paste
- Juice of 1 lime
- Chopped fresh cilantro, for garnish
- Sour cream or Greek yogurt, for serving (optional)
- Shredded cheese, for serving (optional)
- Tortilla chips or crusty bread, for serving (optional)

Instructions:

1. **Sauté vegetables:**
   - Heat olive oil in a large pot or Dutch oven over medium heat. Add chopped onion, minced garlic, diced bell pepper, carrots, celery, and zucchini. Sauté for 5-7 minutes until vegetables are softened.
2. **Add spices:**
   - Stir in chili powder, ground cumin, smoked paprika, dried oregano, cayenne pepper (if using), salt, and pepper. Cook for 1 minute until fragrant.
3. **Add tomatoes and beans:**
   - Add diced tomatoes (with their juices), drained and rinsed beans, and corn kernels to the pot. Stir to combine.
4. **Simmer:**
   - Pour in vegetable broth and tomato paste. Bring the chili to a boil, then reduce the heat to low. Let it simmer uncovered for 20-25 minutes, stirring occasionally, until the chili has thickened and flavors have melded together.

5. **Finish and serve:**
    - Stir in fresh lime juice. Taste and adjust seasoning with salt and pepper if needed.
    - Serve hot, garnished with chopped fresh cilantro. Optionally, top with a dollop of sour cream or Greek yogurt, shredded cheese, and serve with tortilla chips or crusty bread on the side.

Enjoy this comforting and nutritious Vegetarian Chili as a satisfying meal on its own or as a part of a larger spread!

French Onion Soup

Ingredients:

- 4 large yellow onions, thinly sliced
- 2 tablespoons butter
- 2 tablespoons olive oil
- 1 teaspoon sugar (optional, to help with caramelization)
- 2 cloves garlic, minced
- 1/2 cup dry white wine (such as Chardonnay or Sauvignon Blanc)
- 6 cups beef broth (or vegetable broth for a vegetarian version)
- 1 bay leaf
- 1 teaspoon dried thyme (or 2-3 sprigs of fresh thyme)
- Salt and pepper, to taste
- Baguette or French bread, sliced
- 2 cups shredded Gruyère cheese (or Swiss cheese)

Instructions:

1. **Caramelize the onions:**
   - In a large pot or Dutch oven, heat butter and olive oil over medium-low heat. Add thinly sliced onions and cook, stirring occasionally, for about 30-40 minutes until the onions are deeply caramelized and golden brown. If desired, sprinkle sugar over the onions to help with caramelization.
2. **Add garlic and deglaze:**
   - Add minced garlic to the caramelized onions and cook for another 1-2 minutes until fragrant. Pour in the white wine to deglaze the pot, scraping up any browned bits from the bottom with a wooden spoon.
3. **Simmer the soup:**
   - Add beef broth (or vegetable broth), bay leaf, and dried thyme to the pot. Season with salt and pepper to taste. Bring the soup to a simmer over medium heat. Reduce the heat to low and let it simmer gently, uncovered, for 20-30 minutes to allow the flavors to meld together.
4. **Prepare the bread and cheese:**
   - While the soup simmers, preheat your oven's broiler. Arrange the baguette or French bread slices on a baking sheet in a single layer. Toast them under the broiler for 1-2 minutes per side until lightly golden and crispy.
5. **Assemble and serve:**
   - Remove the bay leaf and thyme sprigs (if using) from the soup. Ladle the hot soup into oven-safe bowls or crocks.
   - Place a toasted baguette slice on top of each bowl of soup. Sprinkle shredded Gruyère cheese (or Swiss cheese) generously over the bread and soup.
6. **Broil the soup:**
   - Place the soup bowls on a baking sheet and broil for 2-3 minutes, or until the cheese is melted, bubbly, and golden brown.

7. **Serve hot:**
    - Carefully remove the soup bowls from the oven (they will be hot!). Garnish with additional fresh thyme leaves if desired.
    - Serve immediately, as French Onion Soup is best enjoyed piping hot with gooey melted cheese on top.

Enjoy the rich and comforting flavors of homemade French Onion Soup as a delicious starter or a satisfying main course!

Pad Thai

Ingredients:

- 8 oz (225g) rice noodles (preferably flat rice noodles, about 1/4 inch wide)
- 1/2 lb (225g) medium shrimp, peeled and deveined (optional)
- 2 tablespoons vegetable oil
- 2 cloves garlic, minced
- 1 shallot, finely chopped
- 1/2 cup extra firm tofu, cut into small cubes (optional)
- 2 eggs, lightly beaten
- 1 cup bean sprouts
- 4 green onions (scallions), sliced into 1-inch pieces
- 1/4 cup roasted peanuts, crushed
- Lime wedges, for serving

For the Pad Thai Sauce:

- 3 tablespoons fish sauce (or soy sauce for vegetarian/vegan version)
- 3 tablespoons tamarind paste
- 2 tablespoons palm sugar (or brown sugar)
- 1 tablespoon rice vinegar
- 1/2 teaspoon paprika (optional, for color)
- 1/4 teaspoon crushed red pepper flakes (adjust to taste)

Instructions:

1. **Prepare the rice noodles:**
    - Cook rice noodles according to package instructions until they are al dente. Drain and rinse under cold water to stop cooking. Set aside.
2. **Make the Pad Thai Sauce:**
    - In a small bowl, whisk together fish sauce (or soy sauce), tamarind paste, palm sugar (or brown sugar), rice vinegar, paprika (if using), and crushed red pepper flakes until the sugar dissolves. Adjust the seasoning to your taste.
3. **Prepare the ingredients:**
    - Heat 1 tablespoon of vegetable oil in a large skillet or wok over medium-high heat. Add shrimp (if using) and cook until pink and cooked through, about 2-3 minutes per side. Remove shrimp from the skillet and set aside.
    - In the same skillet, heat another tablespoon of vegetable oil. Add minced garlic and chopped shallot, sauté for 1-2 minutes until fragrant.
4. **Cook the tofu and eggs:**
    - If using tofu, add the cubed tofu to the skillet with garlic and shallot. Cook for 2-3 minutes until lightly browned. Push tofu to one side of the skillet.
    - Pour beaten eggs into the empty side of the skillet. Scramble the eggs until cooked through, then mix them with the tofu and other ingredients in the skillet.

5. **Stir-fry with noodles and sauce:**
   - Add cooked rice noodles and prepared Pad Thai sauce to the skillet. Toss everything together gently to coat the noodles evenly with the sauce.
   - Stir in cooked shrimp (if using), bean sprouts, and sliced green onions (scallions). Cook for 2-3 minutes until heated through.
6. **Serve:**
   - Transfer Pad Thai to serving plates or bowls.
   - Garnish with crushed peanuts and serve with lime wedges on the side.

Enjoy your homemade Pad Thai with its delicious blend of flavors and textures! Adjust the level of spiciness by adding more crushed red pepper flakes or chili flakes if desired.

Beef Tacos

Ingredients:

- 1 lb (450g) ground beef
- 1 tablespoon vegetable oil
- 1 small onion, finely chopped
- 2 cloves garlic, minced
- 1 tablespoon chili powder
- 1 teaspoon ground cumin
- 1/2 teaspoon paprika
- 1/4 teaspoon dried oregano
- Salt and pepper, to taste
- 1/2 cup tomato sauce
- 1/2 cup beef broth or water
- 8-10 small corn or flour tortillas
- Toppings: shredded lettuce, diced tomatoes, shredded cheese, sour cream, salsa, chopped cilantro, lime wedges, etc.

Instructions:

1. **Cook the beef filling:**
   - Heat vegetable oil in a large skillet over medium-high heat. Add chopped onion and cook for 2-3 minutes until softened.
   - Add minced garlic and cook for another 1 minute until fragrant.
   - Add ground beef to the skillet, breaking it up with a spatula. Cook for 5-7 minutes until browned and cooked through.
2. **Season the beef:**
   - Stir in chili powder, ground cumin, paprika, dried oregano, salt, and pepper. Cook for 1-2 minutes until the spices are fragrant.
3. **Add tomato sauce and broth:**
   - Pour in tomato sauce and beef broth (or water). Bring to a simmer and cook for 5-7 minutes until the sauce thickens slightly. Taste and adjust seasoning if needed.
4. **Prepare the tortillas:**
   - While the beef filling simmers, heat a separate skillet over medium heat. Warm each tortilla for about 30 seconds per side until soft and pliable. Stack them and keep warm wrapped in a clean kitchen towel.
5. **Assemble the tacos:**
   - Spoon a portion of the beef filling onto each tortilla.
   - Add your desired toppings such as shredded lettuce, diced tomatoes, shredded cheese, sour cream, salsa, and chopped cilantro.
6. **Serve:**
   - Serve beef tacos hot with lime wedges on the side for squeezing over the tacos.

Enjoy your homemade beef tacos with your favorite toppings for a delicious and satisfying meal!

Baked Salmon with Dill

Ingredients:

- 4 salmon fillets, skin-on or skinless (about 6 oz / 170g each)
- Salt and pepper, to taste
- 2 tablespoons olive oil
- 2 tablespoons fresh dill, chopped
- 2 cloves garlic, minced
- 1 lemon, sliced
- Lemon wedges, for serving

Instructions:

1. **Preheat the oven:**
   - Preheat your oven to 400°F (200°C). Line a baking sheet with parchment paper or lightly grease it with olive oil to prevent sticking.
2. **Prepare the salmon:**
   - Place the salmon fillets on the prepared baking sheet. Season both sides of the salmon with salt and pepper.
3. **Make the dill mixture:**
   - In a small bowl, mix together olive oil, chopped fresh dill, and minced garlic.
4. **Coat the salmon:**
   - Brush the dill mixture evenly over the top of each salmon fillet. Make sure the salmon is well coated with the mixture.
5. **Add lemon slices:**
   - Place a couple of lemon slices on top of each salmon fillet for extra flavor.
6. **Bake the salmon:**
   - Bake the salmon in the preheated oven for 12-15 minutes, depending on the thickness of the fillets. The salmon is done when it flakes easily with a fork and reaches an internal temperature of 145°F (63°C).
7. **Serve:**
   - Remove the baked salmon from the oven and let it rest for a few minutes.
   - Serve hot, garnished with additional fresh dill and lemon wedges on the side.

Enjoy your tender and flavorful Baked Salmon with Dill as a nutritious and delicious main dish! Pair it with steamed vegetables, rice, or a fresh salad for a complete meal.

Greek Salad

Ingredients:

- 1 large cucumber, seeded and sliced
- 4-5 ripe tomatoes, cut into wedges or chunks
- 1 red onion, thinly sliced
- 1 green bell pepper, seeded and sliced
- 1/2 cup Kalamata olives, pitted
- 1/2 cup crumbled feta cheese
- Fresh oregano leaves, for garnish (optional)
- Salt and pepper, to taste

For the dressing:

- 1/4 cup extra virgin olive oil
- 2 tablespoons red wine vinegar
- 1 teaspoon dried oregano
- 1 clove garlic, minced
- Juice of 1/2 lemon
- Salt and pepper, to taste

Instructions:

1. **Prepare the vegetables:**
   - In a large salad bowl, combine cucumber slices, tomato wedges, sliced red onion, and green bell pepper slices.
2. **Add olives and feta:**
   - Add Kalamata olives and crumbled feta cheese to the bowl with the vegetables.
3. **Make the dressing:**
   - In a small bowl, whisk together extra virgin olive oil, red wine vinegar, dried oregano, minced garlic, lemon juice, salt, and pepper until well combined.
4. **Assemble the salad:**
   - Pour the dressing over the salad ingredients in the bowl. Toss gently to coat all the vegetables with the dressing.
5. **Garnish and serve:**
   - Garnish the Greek Salad with fresh oregano leaves, if desired.
   - Serve immediately as a side dish or light meal.

Greek Salad is perfect on its own or as a side to grilled meats or seafood. It's a refreshing and healthy option that bursts with Mediterranean flavors! Adjust the ingredients and seasoning to your preference for a personalized touch.

Mushroom Risotto

Ingredients:

- 1 cup Arborio rice
- 4 cups vegetable or chicken broth (keep warm)
- 2 tablespoons unsalted butter
- 2 tablespoons olive oil
- 1 small onion, finely chopped
- 2 cloves garlic, minced
- 8 oz (225g) mushrooms (such as cremini, shiitake, or button), sliced
- 1/2 cup dry white wine (optional)
- 1/2 cup grated Parmesan cheese, plus extra for serving
- Salt and pepper, to taste
- Fresh parsley or thyme, chopped, for garnish (optional)

Instructions:

1. **Prepare the mushrooms:**
    - In a large skillet or pan, heat 1 tablespoon of butter and 1 tablespoon of olive oil over medium heat.
    - Add sliced mushrooms and cook for 5-7 minutes until they release their moisture and start to brown. Season with salt and pepper to taste. Remove mushrooms from the skillet and set aside.
2. **Make the risotto:**
    - In the same skillet, add the remaining 1 tablespoon of butter and 1 tablespoon of olive oil.
    - Add chopped onion and garlic. Sauté for 2-3 minutes until onion becomes translucent.
3. **Toast the rice:**
    - Add Arborio rice to the skillet. Stir and cook for 1-2 minutes until the rice is lightly toasted and coated with the butter and oil mixture.
4. **Deglaze with wine (optional):**
    - Pour in the white wine (if using). Cook, stirring constantly, until the wine is absorbed by the rice.
5. **Cook the risotto:**
    - Begin adding the warm broth to the rice mixture, one ladleful at a time, stirring frequently. Allow each addition of broth to be absorbed before adding the next ladleful. This process helps release the starch from the rice, giving risotto its creamy texture.
    - Continue cooking and stirring until the rice is creamy and cooked al dente, about 20-25 minutes. You may not need to use all of the broth.
6. **Add mushrooms and cheese:**
    - Stir in the cooked mushrooms and grated Parmesan cheese. Cook for another 1-2 minutes until the cheese melts and the mushrooms are heated through.

7. **Season and serve:**
    - Taste the risotto and adjust seasoning with salt and pepper if needed.
    - Serve Mushroom Risotto hot, garnished with extra grated Parmesan cheese and chopped fresh parsley or thyme if desired.

Enjoy the creamy and flavorful Mushroom Risotto as a satisfying main dish or as a side to complement your favorite meal!

Chicken Parmesan

Ingredients:

- 4 boneless, skinless chicken breasts
- Salt and pepper, to taste
- 1 cup all-purpose flour
- 2 large eggs, beaten
- 1 cup breadcrumbs (Italian seasoned breadcrumbs work well)
- 1/2 cup grated Parmesan cheese
- 1/2 cup shredded mozzarella cheese
- Vegetable oil, for frying
- 2 cups marinara sauce (homemade or store-bought)
- Fresh basil leaves, chopped, for garnish (optional)
- Cooked spaghetti or your favorite pasta, for serving

Instructions:

1. **Prepare the chicken:**
    - Place each chicken breast between two sheets of plastic wrap or parchment paper. Pound them to an even thickness of about 1/2 inch using a meat mallet or rolling pin. This ensures even cooking.
2. **Season and coat the chicken:**
    - Season the chicken breasts with salt and pepper on both sides.
    - Set up a breading station with three shallow bowls: one with flour, one with beaten eggs, and one with a mixture of breadcrumbs and grated Parmesan cheese.
3. **Bread the chicken:**
    - Dredge each chicken breast in flour, shaking off any excess.
    - Dip into the beaten eggs, allowing any excess to drip off.
    - Coat thoroughly with the breadcrumb and Parmesan mixture, pressing gently to adhere.
4. **Fry the chicken:**
    - In a large skillet, heat enough vegetable oil to cover the bottom of the skillet over medium-high heat.
    - Carefully add breaded chicken breasts to the skillet, cooking in batches if necessary to avoid overcrowding. Fry for about 3-4 minutes per side until golden brown and cooked through (internal temperature of 165°F/75°C). Transfer cooked chicken to a paper towel-lined plate to drain excess oil.
5. **Assemble Chicken Parmesan:**
    - Preheat your oven's broiler.
    - Place cooked chicken breasts in a baking dish or oven-proof skillet.
    - Spoon marinara sauce over each chicken breast, covering them generously.
    - Sprinkle shredded mozzarella cheese on top of each chicken breast.
6. **Broil and serve:**

- Place the baking dish under the broiler for 2-3 minutes, or until the cheese is melted and bubbly.
            - Remove from the oven and let it rest for a few minutes.
            - Garnish with chopped fresh basil leaves if desired.
   7. **Serve:**
            - Serve Chicken Parmesan hot, ideally over cooked spaghetti or your favorite pasta, with extra marinara sauce on the side.

Enjoy the crispy and cheesy goodness of homemade Chicken Parmesan with your favorite sides for a comforting and satisfying meal!

Beef and Broccoli Stir Fry

Ingredients:

- 1 lb (450g) flank steak or sirloin steak, thinly sliced against the grain
- 2 cups broccoli florets
- 2 tablespoons vegetable oil, divided
- 3 cloves garlic, minced
- 1 teaspoon fresh ginger, minced
- 1/4 cup low-sodium soy sauce
- 2 tablespoons oyster sauce
- 1 tablespoon hoisin sauce
- 1 tablespoon cornstarch
- 1/2 cup beef broth or water
- 1 tablespoon brown sugar (optional, for a touch of sweetness)
- Cooked white rice, for serving

Instructions:

1. **Marinate the beef:**
    - In a bowl, combine thinly sliced beef with 1 tablespoon of vegetable oil, minced garlic, minced ginger, and a pinch of salt and pepper. Let it marinate for 15-20 minutes at room temperature.
2. **Prepare the sauce:**
    - In a small bowl, whisk together soy sauce, oyster sauce, hoisin sauce, cornstarch, beef broth (or water), and brown sugar (if using). Set aside.
3. **Stir fry the beef and broccoli:**
    - Heat 1 tablespoon of vegetable oil in a large skillet or wok over medium-high heat.
    - Add marinated beef slices in a single layer. Cook for 1-2 minutes without stirring to sear one side. Then stir-fry for another 1-2 minutes until beef is browned and cooked through. Remove beef from the skillet and set aside.
4. **Cook the broccoli:**
    - In the same skillet, add broccoli florets. Stir-fry for 3-4 minutes until broccoli is tender-crisp. If needed, add a splash of water to create steam and help cook the broccoli faster.
5. **Combine beef and broccoli:**
    - Return cooked beef slices to the skillet with the broccoli.
6. **Add the sauce:**
    - Give the prepared sauce a quick stir, then pour it into the skillet with the beef and broccoli. Stir well to coat everything evenly with the sauce.
7. **Finish and serve:**
    - Cook for another 1-2 minutes until the sauce has thickened slightly and everything is heated through.
    - Serve Beef and Broccoli Stir Fry hot over cooked white rice.

Enjoy this savory and flavorful Beef and Broccoli Stir Fry as a delicious and nutritious meal! Adjust the seasoning and thickness of the sauce to suit your taste preferences.

Butternut Squash Soup

Ingredients:

- 1 medium butternut squash (about 2-3 lbs), peeled, seeded, and diced
- 1 tablespoon olive oil
- 1 onion, chopped
- 2 cloves garlic, minced
- 1 carrot, chopped
- 1 celery stalk, chopped
- 4 cups vegetable broth (or chicken broth)
- 1 teaspoon ground cumin
- 1/2 teaspoon ground cinnamon
- 1/4 teaspoon ground nutmeg
- Salt and pepper, to taste
- 1/2 cup heavy cream (optional, for extra creaminess)
- Fresh parsley or chives, chopped, for garnish (optional)

Instructions:

1. **Prepare the butternut squash:**
    - Peel the butternut squash using a vegetable peeler. Cut it in half lengthwise and scoop out the seeds with a spoon. Dice the squash into cubes.
2. **Sauté the aromatics:**
    - In a large pot or Dutch oven, heat olive oil over medium heat. Add chopped onion, minced garlic, chopped carrot, and chopped celery. Sauté for 5-7 minutes until vegetables are softened and onions are translucent.
3. **Cook the squash:**
    - Add diced butternut squash to the pot with the sautéed vegetables. Stir to combine.
4. **Add broth and spices:**
    - Pour in vegetable broth (or chicken broth) until the squash and vegetables are just covered. Add ground cumin, ground cinnamon, and ground nutmeg. Season with salt and pepper to taste.
5. **Simmer the soup:**
    - Bring the mixture to a boil, then reduce the heat to low. Cover and let it simmer for 20-25 minutes, or until the butternut squash is tender and easily pierced with a fork.
6. **Blend the soup:**
    - Remove the pot from heat. Use an immersion blender to blend the soup until smooth and creamy. Alternatively, transfer the soup in batches to a blender and blend until smooth. Be cautious blending hot liquids.
7. **Finish the soup:**
    - If using heavy cream, stir it into the blended soup until well combined. Adjust seasoning with more salt and pepper if needed.

8. **Serve:**
    - Ladle Butternut Squash Soup into bowls. Garnish with chopped fresh parsley or chives if desired.
    - Serve hot and enjoy with crusty bread or a side salad.

This Butternut Squash Soup is creamy, flavorful, and perfect for a cozy meal. It can be made ahead of time and stored in the refrigerator for a few days or frozen for longer storage. Adjust the thickness by adding more broth or cream to suit your preference.

Lasagna

Ingredients:

- 12 lasagna noodles (about 1 lb), cooked according to package instructions
- 1 lb (450g) ground beef or Italian sausage
- 1 onion, finely chopped
- 4 cloves garlic, minced
- 1 can (28 oz / 800g) crushed tomatoes
- 1 can (15 oz / 425g) tomato sauce
- 1/2 cup red wine (optional)
- 2 teaspoons dried basil
- 1 teaspoon dried oregano
- Salt and pepper, to taste
- 2 cups shredded mozzarella cheese
- 1 cup grated Parmesan cheese

For the béchamel sauce:

- 4 tablespoons unsalted butter
- 1/4 cup all-purpose flour
- 4 cups milk (preferably whole milk)
- 1/4 teaspoon ground nutmeg
- Salt and pepper, to taste

Instructions:

1. **Prepare the meat sauce:**
    - In a large skillet or Dutch oven, cook ground beef or Italian sausage over medium-high heat until browned. Break up any large chunks with a wooden spoon.
    - Add chopped onion and minced garlic. Cook for 3-4 minutes until onions are translucent.
    - Stir in crushed tomatoes, tomato sauce, red wine (if using), dried basil, dried oregano, salt, and pepper. Bring to a simmer, then reduce heat to low. Let it simmer uncovered for about 30-40 minutes, stirring occasionally, until the sauce thickens. Taste and adjust seasoning if needed.
2. **Make the béchamel sauce:**
    - In a medium saucepan, melt butter over medium heat. Add flour and whisk continuously for 1-2 minutes until it forms a smooth paste (roux) and starts to bubble.
    - Gradually pour in milk, whisking constantly to prevent lumps from forming. Cook for 5-7 minutes, whisking frequently, until the sauce thickens and coats the back of a spoon.
    - Stir in ground nutmeg, salt, and pepper. Remove from heat and set aside.

3. **Assemble the lasagna:**
    - Preheat your oven to 375°F (190°C). Grease a 9x13-inch baking dish.
    - Spread a thin layer of meat sauce on the bottom of the baking dish.
    - Arrange a layer of cooked lasagna noodles over the meat sauce.
    - Spread a layer of meat sauce over the noodles, followed by a layer of béchamel sauce, and sprinkle with mozzarella and Parmesan cheese.
    - Repeat layers (noodles, meat sauce, béchamel sauce, cheese) until all ingredients are used, finishing with a layer of béchamel sauce and a generous sprinkle of mozzarella and Parmesan cheese on top.
4. **Bake the lasagna:**
    - Cover the baking dish loosely with aluminum foil, tenting it slightly to prevent cheese from sticking.
    - Bake in the preheated oven for 25 minutes.
    - Remove the foil and bake for an additional 15-20 minutes until the cheese is golden brown and bubbly.
5. **Rest and serve:**
    - Let the lasagna rest for 10-15 minutes before slicing and serving. This allows the layers to set and makes it easier to cut into neat portions.
    - Serve hot, garnished with fresh basil or parsley if desired.

Enjoy this homemade lasagna with its rich layers of flavors and textures, perfect for a comforting family meal or special occasion!

Teriyaki Chicken

Ingredients:

- 4 boneless, skinless chicken thighs or breasts, cut into bite-sized pieces
- Salt and pepper, to taste
- 1 tablespoon vegetable oil
- 1/2 cup low-sodium soy sauce
- 1/4 cup water
- 3 tablespoons brown sugar
- 2 tablespoons honey
- 2 cloves garlic, minced
- 1 teaspoon grated fresh ginger (or 1/2 teaspoon ground ginger)
- 1 tablespoon cornstarch mixed with 2 tablespoons water (optional, for thickening)

Instructions:

1. **Prepare the chicken:**
   - Season chicken pieces with salt and pepper to taste.
2. **Make the teriyaki sauce:**
   - In a small saucepan, combine soy sauce, water, brown sugar, honey, minced garlic, and grated ginger. Bring to a simmer over medium heat, stirring occasionally until the sugar dissolves.
3. **Cook the chicken:**
   - Heat vegetable oil in a large skillet or pan over medium-high heat.
   - Add chicken pieces to the skillet and cook for 5-7 minutes, stirring occasionally, until chicken is browned and cooked through.
4. **Simmer with teriyaki sauce:**
   - Pour the prepared teriyaki sauce over the cooked chicken in the skillet. Stir to coat the chicken evenly with the sauce.
5. **Thicken the sauce (optional):**
   - If desired, stir in the cornstarch mixture into the skillet to thicken the sauce. Cook for another 1-2 minutes until the sauce thickens slightly.
6. **Serve:**
   - Remove from heat and let the chicken rest for a few minutes.
   - Serve hot teriyaki chicken over steamed rice or with your favorite vegetables.
   - Garnish with sesame seeds and sliced green onions if desired.

Enjoy this homemade Teriyaki Chicken with its deliciously sticky and flavorful sauce! It's a quick and satisfying dish that's perfect for busy weeknight dinners.

Ratatouille

Ingredients:

- 1 large eggplant, cut into 1-inch cubes
- 2 medium zucchinis, sliced
- 1 large yellow bell pepper, sliced
- 1 large red bell pepper, sliced
- 1 onion, thinly sliced
- 4 cloves garlic, minced
- 4 large tomatoes, chopped (or 1 can of diced tomatoes)
- 2 tablespoons tomato paste
- 1/4 cup olive oil
- 1 teaspoon dried thyme (or 2-3 sprigs of fresh thyme)
- 1 teaspoon dried oregano
- Salt and pepper, to taste
- Fresh basil or parsley, chopped, for garnish (optional)

Instructions:

1. **Prepare the vegetables:**
   - Heat 2 tablespoons of olive oil in a large skillet or Dutch oven over medium heat.
   - Add sliced onion and minced garlic. Sauté for 2-3 minutes until onions are translucent.
2. **Cook the eggplant:**
   - Add cubed eggplant to the skillet. Cook for 5-7 minutes, stirring occasionally, until eggplant starts to soften and brown slightly.
3. **Add peppers and zucchini:**
   - Add sliced yellow and red bell peppers, and sliced zucchini to the skillet. Stir to combine with the eggplant and onions.
4. **Prepare the tomato sauce:**
   - Add chopped tomatoes (or canned diced tomatoes) and tomato paste to the skillet.
   - Season with dried thyme, dried oregano, salt, and pepper. Stir well to combine all ingredients.
5. **Simmer the ratatouille:**
   - Reduce heat to low and let the ratatouille simmer gently for 20-25 minutes, stirring occasionally, until vegetables are tender and flavors meld together. If the mixture becomes too dry, add a splash of water or vegetable broth.
6. **Adjust seasoning and serve:**
   - Taste and adjust seasoning with salt and pepper if needed.
   - Remove from heat and let it rest for a few minutes before serving.
   - Garnish with chopped fresh basil or parsley if desired.
7. **Serve:**

- Serve ratatouille warm as a side dish or a main course. It pairs well with crusty bread, rice, or pasta.

Enjoy this hearty and flavorful Ratatouille as a taste of traditional French cuisine, showcasing the vibrant flavors of summer vegetables!

Pulled Pork Sandwiches

Ingredients:

- 3-4 lbs (1.5-2 kg) pork shoulder or pork butt
- Salt and pepper, to taste
- 1 tablespoon smoked paprika
- 1 tablespoon garlic powder
- 1 tablespoon onion powder
- 1 tablespoon brown sugar
- 1 teaspoon cayenne pepper (optional, for heat)
- 1 cup BBQ sauce (plus extra for serving)
- 1/2 cup chicken broth or water
- Sandwich buns or rolls, for serving
- Coleslaw, pickles, or other toppings (optional)

Instructions:

1. **Prepare the pork:**
    - Pat dry the pork shoulder or pork butt with paper towels. Season generously with salt and pepper.
2. **Season the pork:**
    - In a small bowl, combine smoked paprika, garlic powder, onion powder, brown sugar, and cayenne pepper (if using). Rub the spice mixture all over the pork, coating it evenly.
3. **Slow cook the pork:**
    - Place the seasoned pork in a slow cooker. Pour chicken broth (or water) around the pork.
    - Cover and cook on low for 8-10 hours or on high for 4-6 hours, until the pork is very tender and easily pulls apart with a fork.
4. **Shred the pork:**
    - Remove the cooked pork from the slow cooker and place it on a cutting board or large plate. Use two forks to shred the pork into bite-sized pieces. Discard any excess fat.
5. **Add BBQ sauce:**
    - In a large bowl, combine the shredded pork with BBQ sauce. Mix well to coat the pork evenly. Adjust the amount of BBQ sauce to your preference.
6. **Assemble the sandwiches:**
    - Toast sandwich buns or rolls if desired.
    - Place a generous amount of pulled pork on the bottom half of each bun.
    - Top with additional BBQ sauce, coleslaw, pickles, or other toppings as desired.
7. **Serve:**
    - Serve pulled pork sandwiches immediately, accompanied by your favorite sides like potato salad, cornbread, or fries.

Enjoy these delicious pulled pork sandwiches, packed with smoky, tender pork and savory BBQ flavors! They're perfect for a crowd or a casual family dinner.

Caesar Salad

Ingredients:

For the salad:

- 1 large head of romaine lettuce, washed and torn into bite-sized pieces
- 1 cup croutons (store-bought or homemade)
- 1/2 cup grated Parmesan cheese

For the dressing:

- 1/2 cup mayonnaise
- 2 tablespoons freshly squeezed lemon juice
- 2 tablespoons grated Parmesan cheese
- 1 tablespoon Dijon mustard
- 1 clove garlic, minced
- 1/2 teaspoon Worcestershire sauce
- Salt and freshly ground black pepper, to taste
- 2-3 tablespoons olive oil (optional, for a thinner dressing)

Instructions:

1. **Prepare the dressing:**
   - In a small bowl, whisk together mayonnaise, lemon juice, grated Parmesan cheese, Dijon mustard, minced garlic, Worcestershire sauce, salt, and pepper until well combined.
   - If desired, whisk in olive oil gradually to achieve a thinner consistency. Taste and adjust seasoning as needed.
2. **Assemble the salad:**
   - In a large salad bowl, add torn romaine lettuce leaves.
   - Drizzle Caesar dressing over the lettuce. Toss gently to coat the lettuce evenly with the dressing.
   - Add croutons to the salad bowl and toss again lightly.
3. **Serve:**
   - Transfer the Caesar Salad to serving plates or bowls.
   - Sprinkle grated Parmesan cheese on top of each serving.
   - Optionally, garnish with additional croutons and freshly ground black pepper.
4. **Optional additions:**
   - For a heartier salad, you can add grilled chicken breast slices, cooked shrimp, or even crispy bacon.
5. **Tips:**
   - For homemade croutons, cube day-old bread, toss with olive oil, salt, and pepper, then bake in a preheated oven at 375°F (190°C) until golden brown and crisp.

- Adjust the amount of dressing according to your preference; you may not need all of it for the salad.

Enjoy this classic Caesar Salad as a delicious side dish or a light meal on its own. It's fresh, flavorful, and perfect for any occasion!

Beef Bourguignon

Ingredients:

- 2 lbs (900g) beef chuck or stewing beef, cut into 2-inch cubes
- Salt and pepper, to taste
- 2 tablespoons olive oil
- 4 oz (120g) bacon, chopped
- 1 onion, chopped
- 2 carrots, peeled and sliced
- 2 cloves garlic, minced
- 1 tablespoon tomato paste
- 2 cups red wine (Burgundy or any dry red wine)
- 2 cups beef broth
- 1 bouquet garni (a bundle of herbs such as thyme, parsley, and bay leaf tied together with kitchen twine)
- 8 oz (225g) mushrooms, quartered
- 1 tablespoon butter
- Chopped fresh parsley, for garnish (optional)

Instructions:

1. **Prepare the beef:**
   - Season beef cubes with salt and pepper.
   - Heat olive oil in a large Dutch oven or heavy-bottomed pot over medium-high heat. Brown the beef in batches until well-browned on all sides. Transfer browned beef to a plate and set aside.
2. **Cook the bacon and vegetables:**
   - In the same pot, add chopped bacon and cook until crisp. Remove bacon with a slotted spoon and set aside.
   - Add chopped onion, sliced carrots, and minced garlic to the pot. Sauté for 5-7 minutes until onions are softened.
3. **Deglaze the pot:**
   - Stir in tomato paste and cook for 1 minute.
   - Pour in red wine, scraping up any browned bits from the bottom of the pot (deglazing). Bring to a boil and cook for 5 minutes to reduce slightly.
4. **Simmer the stew:**
   - Return the browned beef and cooked bacon to the pot.
   - Add beef broth and bouquet garni. Bring to a simmer, then cover and cook over low heat for 2-3 hours, or until beef is very tender. Stir occasionally.
5. **Sauté the mushrooms:**
   - In a separate skillet, melt butter over medium heat. Add quartered mushrooms and sauté until they release their moisture and turn golden brown, about 5-7 minutes.
6. **Finish the stew:**

- Add sautéed mushrooms to the pot with the beef stew during the last 30 minutes of cooking.
- Taste and adjust seasoning with salt and pepper if needed.

7. **Serve:**
    - Remove bouquet garni from the stew.
    - Serve Beef Bourguignon hot, garnished with chopped fresh parsley if desired.
    - Enjoy with crusty bread, mashed potatoes, or over egg noodles.

Beef Bourguignon is best when allowed to sit for a while before serving, as the flavors meld together beautifully. It's a perfect dish for special occasions or cozy family dinners!

Stuffed Bell Peppers

Ingredients:

- 6 large bell peppers (any color), tops cut off and seeds removed
- 1 lb (450g) ground beef or turkey
- 1 onion, finely chopped
- 2 cloves garlic, minced
- 1 cup cooked rice (white or brown)
- 1 can (14.5 oz / 400g) diced tomatoes, drained
- 1 cup shredded cheese (such as mozzarella, cheddar, or a blend), divided
- 1 teaspoon dried oregano
- 1 teaspoon dried basil
- Salt and pepper, to taste
- Fresh parsley, chopped, for garnish (optional)

Instructions:

1. **Preheat the oven:**
    - Preheat your oven to 350°F (175°C).
2. **Prepare the bell peppers:**
    - Cut the tops off the bell peppers and remove the seeds and membranes inside. Rinse the peppers under cold water.
3. **Cook the filling:**
    - In a large skillet, cook ground beef (or turkey) over medium-high heat until browned. Break up any large chunks with a spoon.
    - Add chopped onion and minced garlic to the skillet. Cook for 2-3 minutes until onions are translucent.
    - Stir in cooked rice, drained diced tomatoes, 1/2 cup of shredded cheese, dried oregano, dried basil, salt, and pepper. Mix well to combine and cook for another 2-3 minutes.
4. **Stuff the peppers:**
    - Place the hollowed-out bell peppers upright in a baking dish.
    - Spoon the filling mixture into each bell pepper, pressing gently to pack it in.
    - Top each stuffed pepper with the remaining shredded cheese.
5. **Bake the stuffed peppers:**
    - Cover the baking dish loosely with aluminum foil.
    - Bake in the preheated oven for 30-35 minutes, or until the peppers are tender and the filling is heated through.
6. **Serve:**
    - Remove the stuffed bell peppers from the oven.
    - Garnish with chopped fresh parsley if desired.
    - Serve hot as a main dish. They can be accompanied by a side salad or crusty bread.

Enjoy these hearty and flavorful stuffed bell peppers as a satisfying meal that's both comforting and nutritious!

Chicken Enchiladas

Ingredients:

- 1 lb (450g) boneless, skinless chicken breasts or thighs
- Salt and pepper, to taste
- 1 tablespoon olive oil
- 1 onion, finely chopped
- 2 cloves garlic, minced
- 1 teaspoon ground cumin
- 1 teaspoon chili powder
- 1/2 teaspoon smoked paprika
- 1 can (14 oz / 400g) diced tomatoes, drained
- 1 can (4 oz / 113g) chopped green chilies
- 1/2 cup chicken broth
- 1/2 cup sour cream
- 2 cups shredded cheese (such as Monterey Jack, cheddar, or a blend), divided
- 8-10 large flour tortillas (or corn tortillas, if preferred)
- 1 can (10 oz / 283g) red enchilada sauce
- Fresh cilantro, chopped, for garnish (optional)
- Sliced jalapeños, for garnish (optional)

Instructions:

1. **Cook the chicken:**
    - Season chicken breasts or thighs with salt and pepper.
    - Heat olive oil in a large skillet over medium-high heat. Cook chicken until browned on both sides and cooked through, about 6-8 minutes per side, depending on thickness. Remove from skillet and let it cool slightly. Shred the chicken using two forks.
2. **Prepare the filling:**
    - In the same skillet, add chopped onion and cook until softened, about 3-4 minutes.
    - Add minced garlic, ground cumin, chili powder, and smoked paprika. Cook for 1 minute until fragrant.
    - Stir in diced tomatoes, chopped green chilies, and chicken broth. Bring to a simmer and cook for 5 minutes.
    - Remove from heat and stir in sour cream and 1 cup of shredded cheese until cheese is melted.
    - Add shredded chicken to the skillet and mix well to combine.
3. **Assemble the enchiladas:**
    - Preheat your oven to 350°F (175°C).
    - Spread a thin layer of enchilada sauce on the bottom of a baking dish.
    - Spoon chicken filling evenly down the center of each tortilla. Roll up tightly and place seam-side down in the baking dish.

- Repeat with remaining tortillas and filling.
4. **Bake the enchiladas:**
    - Pour remaining enchilada sauce over the rolled tortillas in the baking dish.
    - Sprinkle remaining 1 cup of shredded cheese over the top.
    - Cover the baking dish with aluminum foil and bake in the preheated oven for 20-25 minutes, until the enchiladas are heated through and cheese is melted.
5. **Serve:**
    - Remove from oven and let it rest for a few minutes.
    - Garnish with chopped fresh cilantro and sliced jalapeños if desired.
    - Serve hot, with optional sides like Mexican rice, refried beans, guacamole, or salsa.

Enjoy these delicious chicken enchiladas, filled with savory flavors and topped with melted cheese and enchilada sauce! They're perfect for a family dinner or entertaining guests.

Quiche Lorraine

Ingredients:

For the crust:

- 1 1/4 cups all-purpose flour
- 1/2 teaspoon salt
- 1/2 cup cold unsalted butter, cut into small cubes
- 3-4 tablespoons ice water

For the filling:

- 6 slices bacon, cooked until crispy and chopped
- 1 cup shredded Gruyère cheese (or Swiss cheese)
- 4 large eggs
- 1 cup heavy cream (or half-and-half)
- 1/2 cup whole milk
- 1/4 teaspoon salt
- 1/4 teaspoon black pepper
- Pinch of nutmeg (optional)
- Chopped fresh chives or parsley, for garnish (optional)

Instructions:

1. **Make the crust:**
    - In a food processor, combine flour and salt. Add cold cubed butter and pulse until mixture resembles coarse crumbs.
    - Gradually add ice water, 1 tablespoon at a time, pulsing until dough begins to come together. Be careful not to overmix.
    - Turn dough out onto a lightly floured surface and shape into a disk. Wrap in plastic wrap and refrigerate for at least 1 hour, or overnight.
2. **Preheat oven and prepare pan:**
    - Preheat your oven to 375°F (190°C).
    - Roll out chilled dough on a lightly floured surface to fit a 9-inch tart pan with removable bottom. Press dough into the bottom and up the sides of the pan. Trim excess dough. Prick the bottom of the crust with a fork.
3. **Blind bake the crust:**
    - Line the crust with parchment paper and fill with pie weights or dried beans.
    - Bake in preheated oven for 15 minutes. Remove parchment paper and weights, then bake for an additional 5 minutes until crust is golden brown. Remove from oven and let it cool slightly.
4. **Prepare the filling:**
    - Scatter chopped bacon and shredded cheese evenly over the bottom of the partially baked crust.

5. **Make the custard:**
    - In a mixing bowl, whisk together eggs, heavy cream, milk, salt, pepper, and nutmeg (if using) until well combined.
6. **Assemble and bake:**
    - Pour custard mixture over the bacon and cheese in the tart shell.
    - Place the tart pan on a baking sheet and bake in the preheated oven for 30-35 minutes, or until the custard is set and the top is golden brown.
7. **Serve:**
    - Remove Quiche Lorraine from the oven and let it cool for 10-15 minutes before slicing.
    - Garnish with chopped fresh chives or parsley if desired.
    - Serve warm or at room temperature as a delicious appetizer, brunch dish, or light meal.

Enjoy this classic Quiche Lorraine with its rich, creamy filling and savory bacon flavor, encased in a crisp buttery crust!

Thai Green Curry

Ingredients:

For the Green Curry Paste:

- 2 green Thai chilies, chopped (adjust to taste for spiciness)
- 2 shallots, chopped
- 4 cloves garlic, chopped
- 1 stalk lemongrass, chopped (tender part only)
- 1-inch piece of galangal or ginger, chopped
- 1 tablespoon chopped cilantro stems
- 1 tablespoon chopped fresh coriander (cilantro) leaves
- 1 teaspoon ground cumin
- 1 teaspoon ground coriander
- 1/2 teaspoon ground white pepper
- Zest of 1 lime
- 1 tablespoon shrimp paste (optional, for authenticity)
- 2 tablespoons vegetable oil

For the Curry:

- 1 tablespoon vegetable oil
- 1 lb (450g) chicken, beef, shrimp, tofu, or vegetables (cut into bite-sized pieces)
- 1 can (14 oz / 400ml) coconut milk
- 1 cup chicken or vegetable broth
- 2 tablespoons fish sauce (or soy sauce for vegetarian)
- 1 tablespoon palm sugar or brown sugar
- 1 red bell pepper, sliced
- 1 cup bamboo shoots, drained (optional)
- 1 cup Thai basil leaves, torn
- Lime wedges, for serving
- Cooked jasmine rice, for serving

Instructions:

1. **Make the Green Curry Paste:**
   - In a blender or food processor, combine green Thai chilies, shallots, garlic, lemongrass, galangal (or ginger), cilantro stems, coriander leaves, ground cumin, ground coriander, ground white pepper, lime zest, and shrimp paste (if using).
   - Blend until a smooth paste forms, adding vegetable oil gradually to help with blending.
2. **Prepare the Curry:**
   - Heat vegetable oil in a large pot or wok over medium heat.

- Add 2-3 tablespoons of the green curry paste (store any remaining paste in an airtight container in the refrigerator for up to a week or freeze for longer storage).
- Cook the curry paste for 1-2 minutes, stirring constantly, until fragrant.

3. **Cook the protein and vegetables:**
   - Add your choice of protein (chicken, beef, shrimp, tofu) to the pot. Cook until the protein is browned or cooked through.
   - Pour in coconut milk and chicken or vegetable broth. Stir to combine.

4. **Simmer the curry:**
   - Bring the curry to a simmer. Add fish sauce (or soy sauce for vegetarian), palm sugar (or brown sugar), sliced red bell pepper, and bamboo shoots (if using).
   - Let the curry simmer gently for 10-15 minutes, stirring occasionally, until the vegetables are tender and the flavors have melded.

5. **Finish and serve:**
   - Remove the curry from heat. Stir in torn Thai basil leaves.
   - Taste and adjust seasoning with more fish sauce (or soy sauce) and sugar if needed.
   - Serve hot Thai Green Curry over cooked jasmine rice.
   - Garnish with additional Thai basil leaves and serve with lime wedges on the side.

Enjoy this flavorful and aromatic Thai Green Curry, packed with delicious Thai spices and creamy coconut milk. It's perfect for a satisfying meal that brings a taste of Thailand to your table!

Eggplant Parmesan

Ingredients:

- 2 large eggplants, sliced into 1/2-inch rounds
- Salt, for sprinkling
- 1 cup all-purpose flour
- 3 large eggs, beaten
- 2 cups breadcrumbs (plain or seasoned)
- 1 cup grated Parmesan cheese
- Vegetable oil, for frying
- 4 cups marinara sauce (homemade or store-bought)
- 2 cups shredded mozzarella cheese
- 1/2 cup chopped fresh basil or parsley, for garnish (optional)

Instructions:

1. **Prepare the eggplant:**
    - Place eggplant slices on a baking sheet lined with paper towels. Sprinkle both sides generously with salt and let them sit for about 30 minutes to draw out excess moisture. Pat dry with paper towels.
2. **Set up breading station:**
    - Prepare three shallow bowls: one with flour, one with beaten eggs, and one with a mixture of breadcrumbs and grated Parmesan cheese.
3. **Bread the eggplant:**
    - Dredge each eggplant slice in flour, shaking off excess.
    - Dip in beaten eggs, allowing excess to drip off.
    - Coat thoroughly in breadcrumb-Parmesan mixture, pressing gently to adhere. Repeat with all slices.
4. **Fry the eggplant:**
    - In a large skillet, heat vegetable oil over medium-high heat until shimmering.
    - Fry breaded eggplant slices in batches, turning once, until golden brown and crispy, about 2-3 minutes per side. Transfer to a paper towel-lined plate to drain excess oil.
5. **Assemble Eggplant Parmesan:**
    - Preheat your oven to 375°F (190°C).
    - Spread a thin layer of marinara sauce on the bottom of a 9x13-inch baking dish.
    - Arrange a layer of fried eggplant slices in the dish, overlapping slightly if needed.
    - Spoon more marinara sauce over the eggplant, spreading evenly.
    - Sprinkle shredded mozzarella cheese over the sauce.
    - Repeat layers of eggplant, marinara sauce, and mozzarella until all ingredients are used, ending with a layer of sauce and mozzarella on top.
6. **Bake:**
    - Cover the baking dish loosely with aluminum foil and bake in the preheated oven for 25-30 minutes, until the cheese is melted and bubbly.

7. **Serve:**
   - Remove from the oven and let it cool slightly before serving.
   - Garnish with chopped fresh basil or parsley if desired.
   - Serve hot Eggplant Parmesan as a main dish, accompanied by a side of pasta or crusty bread.

Enjoy this comforting and flavorful Eggplant Parmesan, with its crispy texture, gooey cheese, and rich marinara sauce. It's a perfect dish for a hearty family dinner or for entertaining guests!

Paella

Ingredients:

- 1 lb (450g) chicken thighs or breasts, cut into bite-sized pieces
- 1 lb (450g) Spanish chorizo sausage, sliced
- 1 lb (450g) large shrimp (prawns), peeled and deveined
- 1 onion, diced
- 4 cloves garlic, minced
- 1 red bell pepper, sliced
- 1 yellow bell pepper, sliced
- 1 cup green beans, trimmed and halved
- 1 cup frozen peas
- 2 cups Bomba or Arborio rice
- 4 cups chicken broth
- 1 teaspoon saffron threads, steeped in 1/4 cup hot water
- 1 teaspoon smoked paprika
- Salt and pepper, to taste
- Olive oil
- Lemon wedges, for serving
- Chopped fresh parsley, for garnish

Instructions:

1. **Prepare the ingredients:**
    - Season chicken pieces with salt and pepper.
    - Heat olive oil in a large paella pan or a wide skillet over medium-high heat. Brown chicken pieces on all sides. Remove and set aside.
2. **Cook the chorizo and vegetables:**
    - Add chorizo slices to the pan and cook until browned and slightly crispy. Remove and set aside.
    - In the same pan, sauté diced onion and minced garlic until softened.
    - Add sliced bell peppers and green beans. Cook for a few minutes until vegetables start to soften.
3. **Add rice and broth:**
    - Stir in Bomba or Arborio rice and cook for 1-2 minutes, stirring constantly, until rice is coated with oil and slightly translucent.
    - Pour in chicken broth, saffron-infused water, and smoked paprika. Stir to combine.
4. **Simmer the paella:**
    - Arrange chicken pieces and chorizo slices evenly over the rice mixture.
    - Bring to a boil, then reduce heat to medium-low. Simmer uncovered for about 15-20 minutes, without stirring, until most of the liquid is absorbed and rice is almost tender. Add more broth if needed to keep the rice moist.
5. **Add shrimp and peas:**

- Nestle shrimp and frozen peas into the rice mixture.
- Cover with foil or a lid and cook for another 5-10 minutes, until shrimp are pink and cooked through and rice is tender. Remove from heat.

6. **Rest and serve:**
    - Let the paella rest, covered, for 5-10 minutes to allow flavors to meld and excess liquid to be absorbed.
    - Garnish with chopped parsley and serve with lemon wedges on the side.

7. **Serve hot:**
    - Serve paella directly from the pan, offering lemon wedges for squeezing over individual servings.

Enjoy this delicious and vibrant Spanish Paella, filled with a mix of meats, seafood, and vegetables, all infused with saffron and smoked paprika flavors. It's a wonderful dish for sharing with family and friends!

Tandoori Chicken

Ingredients:

- 4 bone-in, skinless chicken thighs or 8 bone-in, skinless chicken drumsticks
- 1 cup plain yogurt (Greek yogurt works well)
- 2 tablespoons lemon juice
- 3 cloves garlic, minced
- 1-inch piece of ginger, grated or minced
- 2 teaspoons ground cumin
- 2 teaspoons ground coriander
- 2 teaspoons paprika
- 1 teaspoon turmeric
- 1 teaspoon cayenne pepper (adjust to taste for spiciness)
- 1 teaspoon garam masala
- 1 teaspoon salt, or to taste
- 1/2 teaspoon black pepper
- 2 tablespoons vegetable oil
- Fresh cilantro or parsley, chopped, for garnish
- Lemon wedges, for serving

Instructions:

1. **Prepare the marinade:**
    - In a large bowl, combine yogurt, lemon juice, minced garlic, grated ginger, ground cumin, ground coriander, paprika, turmeric, cayenne pepper, garam masala, salt, black pepper, and vegetable oil. Mix well until smooth.
2. **Marinate the chicken:**
    - Score the chicken pieces with a sharp knife to allow the marinade to penetrate.
    - Add chicken pieces to the marinade, turning to coat each piece thoroughly. Cover the bowl with plastic wrap and refrigerate for at least 2 hours, or preferably overnight for the flavors to develop.
3. **Preheat the oven or grill:**
    - If using an oven, preheat to 425°F (220°C). If using a grill, preheat to medium-high heat.
4. **Cook the chicken:**
    - If using an oven, line a baking sheet with aluminum foil and place a wire rack on top. Arrange the marinated chicken pieces on the wire rack, leaving space between each piece.
    - Bake in the preheated oven for 25-30 minutes, or until the chicken is cooked through and the juices run clear. You can also broil for a few minutes at the end for a charred effect.
    - If using a grill, grill the chicken pieces for about 6-8 minutes per side, or until cooked through and charred in spots. Use a meat thermometer to ensure the internal temperature of the chicken reaches 165°F (75°C).

5. **Serve:**
    - Remove the Tandoori Chicken from the oven or grill.
    - Sprinkle with chopped fresh cilantro or parsley.
    - Serve hot with lemon wedges on the side for squeezing over the chicken.

Tandoori Chicken pairs well with naan bread, rice, or a fresh salad. It's a flavorful and aromatic dish that brings the taste of Indian cuisine to your table!

Corn Chowder

Ingredients:

- 4 slices bacon, chopped (optional)
- 1 onion, diced
- 2 garlic cloves, minced
- 2 medium potatoes, peeled and diced
- 4 cups fresh or frozen corn kernels (about 4-5 ears of corn)
- 4 cups chicken or vegetable broth
- 1 cup heavy cream or half-and-half
- 1 teaspoon fresh thyme leaves (or 1/2 teaspoon dried thyme)
- Salt and pepper, to taste
- Chopped fresh parsley or chives, for garnish (optional)

Instructions:

1. **Cook the bacon (if using):**
   - In a large pot or Dutch oven, cook chopped bacon over medium heat until crispy. Remove bacon with a slotted spoon and set aside on a paper towel-lined plate.
2. **Sauté onions and garlic:**
   - If not using bacon, heat 2 tablespoons of olive oil or butter in the pot over medium heat. Add diced onions and cook until softened, about 5-7 minutes. Add minced garlic and cook for another minute until fragrant.
3. **Add potatoes and corn:**
   - Add diced potatoes and corn kernels to the pot. Stir to combine with onions and garlic.
4. **Simmer the chowder:**
   - Pour in chicken or vegetable broth. Bring to a boil, then reduce heat to medium-low and simmer uncovered for about 15-20 minutes, or until potatoes are tender.
5. **Blend a portion of the chowder (optional):**
   - For a creamier texture, use an immersion blender to blend a portion of the chowder directly in the pot. Alternatively, transfer about 2 cups of the chowder to a blender and blend until smooth. Return blended mixture to the pot.
6. **Add cream and seasonings:**
   - Stir in heavy cream or half-and-half. Add fresh thyme leaves (or dried thyme). Season with salt and pepper to taste.
7. **Finish and serve:**
   - Simmer the chowder for another 5 minutes to heat through and allow flavors to meld.
   - Ladle corn chowder into bowls. Garnish with crispy bacon (if using), chopped fresh parsley or chives, and additional black pepper if desired.
   - Serve hot with crusty bread or oyster crackers.

Enjoy this creamy and satisfying corn chowder as a comforting meal, perfect for chilly days or whenever you're craving a hearty soup!

Beef Wellington

Ingredients:

- 1 1/2 lb (680g) beef tenderloin, trimmed
- Salt and pepper, to taste
- 2 tablespoons olive oil
- 1 tablespoon Dijon mustard
- 8 oz (225g) mushrooms, finely chopped (such as cremini or button mushrooms)
- 2 cloves garlic, minced
- 1 tablespoon fresh thyme leaves (or 1 teaspoon dried thyme)
- 2 tablespoons butter
- 1/2 cup dry white wine or beef broth
- 1 sheet puff pastry, thawed if frozen
- 1 egg, beaten (for egg wash)
- Salt and pepper, to taste

Instructions:

1. **Prepare the beef:**
    - Season the beef tenderloin generously with salt and pepper.
    - Heat olive oil in a large skillet over high heat. Sear the beef on all sides until well-browned, about 2-3 minutes per side. Remove from heat and let it cool. Brush the seared beef with Dijon mustard and set aside to cool completely.
2. **Make the mushroom duxelles:**
    - In the same skillet, melt butter over medium heat. Add finely chopped mushrooms, garlic, and thyme. Cook, stirring occasionally, until mushrooms release their moisture and turn golden brown, about 8-10 minutes.
    - Add white wine or beef broth to deglaze the skillet, scraping up any browned bits from the bottom. Cook until liquid has evaporated. Season with salt and pepper to taste. Remove from heat and let cool slightly.
3. **Assemble the Beef Wellington:**
    - Roll out the puff pastry on a lightly floured surface to a size large enough to wrap around the beef tenderloin.
    - Spread the mushroom mixture evenly over the puff pastry.
    - Place the seared beef tenderloin in the center of the pastry on top of the mushroom mixture.
4. **Wrap and chill:**
    - Carefully fold the puff pastry over the beef, sealing the edges. Trim any excess pastry if necessary.
    - Transfer the wrapped beef Wellington to a baking sheet lined with parchment paper, seam-side down.
    - Brush the pastry with beaten egg wash.
5. **Bake:**
    - Preheat your oven to 400°F (200°C).

- Bake the Beef Wellington for 35-40 minutes, or until the pastry is golden brown and the internal temperature of the beef reaches 125-130°F (52-55°C) for medium-rare, or until your desired doneness.
- Remove from the oven and let it rest for 10 minutes before slicing.

6. **Serve:**
    - Slice the Beef Wellington into thick slices and serve immediately.
    - You can garnish with fresh herbs and serve with a side of vegetables or mashed potatoes.

Enjoy this elegant and flavorful Beef Wellington, perfect for a special dinner party or celebration!

Baked Ziti

Ingredients:

- 1 lb (450g) ziti pasta (or any short pasta like penne or rigatoni)
- 1 lb (450g) Italian sausage or ground beef (optional)
- 1 onion, diced
- 4 cloves garlic, minced
- 1 jar (24 oz / 680g) marinara sauce
- 1 teaspoon dried oregano
- 1 teaspoon dried basil
- 1/2 teaspoon red pepper flakes (optional, for heat)
- Salt and pepper, to taste
- 15 oz (425g) ricotta cheese
- 1 cup shredded mozzarella cheese
- 1 cup shredded Parmesan cheese, divided
- Fresh basil or parsley, chopped, for garnish (optional)

Instructions:

1. **Preheat the oven:**
   - Preheat your oven to 375°F (190°C). Lightly grease a 9x13-inch baking dish with cooking spray or butter.
2. **Cook the pasta:**
   - Cook the ziti pasta in a large pot of salted boiling water according to package instructions until al dente. Drain and set aside.
3. **Prepare the sauce:**
   - In a large skillet, cook Italian sausage or ground beef over medium-high heat until browned and cooked through. If using sausage, remove from casings before cooking.
   - Add diced onion to the skillet and cook until softened, about 5 minutes. Add minced garlic and cook for another minute until fragrant.
   - Stir in marinara sauce, dried oregano, dried basil, red pepper flakes (if using), salt, and pepper. Simmer for 5-10 minutes to allow flavors to meld.
4. **Combine the pasta and sauce:**
   - In a large mixing bowl, combine cooked ziti pasta and marinara sauce mixture. Mix until pasta is evenly coated.
5. **Assemble the baked ziti:**
   - Spread half of the pasta mixture into the prepared baking dish.
   - Dollop half of the ricotta cheese over the pasta in small spoonfuls. Sprinkle half of the shredded mozzarella cheese and half of the shredded Parmesan cheese over the top.
   - Repeat layers with the remaining pasta mixture, ricotta cheese, mozzarella cheese, and Parmesan cheese.
6. **Bake:**

- Cover the baking dish with aluminum foil and bake in the preheated oven for 20 minutes.
- Remove foil and bake for an additional 10-15 minutes, or until cheese is melted and bubbly.

7. **Serve:**
    - Remove baked ziti from the oven and let it cool for a few minutes.
    - Garnish with chopped fresh basil or parsley, if desired.
    - Serve hot, portioning onto plates or bowls.

Enjoy this comforting and cheesy baked ziti with a side of garlic bread or a fresh green salad for a complete meal!

Caprese Salad

Ingredients:

- 2 large ripe tomatoes, sliced into 1/4-inch thick rounds
- 1 lb (about 450g) fresh mozzarella cheese, sliced into 1/4-inch thick rounds
- Fresh basil leaves
- Extra virgin olive oil
- Balsamic glaze (optional)
- Salt and pepper, to taste

Instructions:

1. **Arrange the salad:**
   - On a large serving platter or individual plates, alternate slices of tomato and mozzarella cheese, overlapping slightly.
2. **Add basil leaves:**
   - Tuck fresh basil leaves between the slices of tomato and mozzarella. You can use whole leaves or tear them into smaller pieces.
3. **Season:**
   - Drizzle extra virgin olive oil over the salad. You can be generous with the olive oil as it adds flavor.
   - Season with salt and pepper to taste. Remember that the mozzarella is usually mildly salty, so adjust accordingly.
4. **Optional garnish:**
   - Drizzle balsamic glaze over the salad for a touch of sweetness and added flavor. Balsamic glaze is a thicker, sweeter version of balsamic vinegar.
5. **Serve:**
   - Serve the Caprese salad immediately, while the ingredients are fresh and flavors are vibrant.

Caprese salad is best enjoyed as a starter or side dish, accompanied by crusty bread or served alongside grilled meats or seafood. It's a wonderful dish to celebrate the flavors of summer with minimal preparation and maximum taste!

Chicken Satay

Ingredients:

For the Chicken Satay:

- 1 lb (450g) boneless, skinless chicken thighs or breasts, cut into thin strips
- Wooden skewers, soaked in water for at least 30 minutes (or use metal skewers)

For the Marinade:

- 3 tablespoons soy sauce
- 2 tablespoons fish sauce
- 2 tablespoons brown sugar
- 2 cloves garlic, minced
- 1 teaspoon ground coriander
- 1 teaspoon ground cumin
- 1/2 teaspoon turmeric
- 1/2 teaspoon ground ginger
- 1 tablespoon vegetable oil

For the Peanut Sauce:

- 1/2 cup creamy peanut butter
- 1/4 cup coconut milk
- 2 tablespoons soy sauce
- 1 tablespoon brown sugar
- 1 tablespoon lime juice
- 1 clove garlic, minced
- 1/2 teaspoon red pepper flakes (adjust to taste)
- Water, as needed to thin the sauce

Instructions:

1. **Prepare the Marinade:**
   - In a bowl, whisk together soy sauce, fish sauce, brown sugar, minced garlic, ground coriander, ground cumin, turmeric, ground ginger, and vegetable oil.
2. **Marinate the Chicken:**
   - Place the chicken strips in a shallow dish or resealable plastic bag. Pour the marinade over the chicken, making sure all pieces are coated. Cover or seal and refrigerate for at least 1 hour, or overnight for best flavor.
3. **Make the Peanut Sauce:**
   - In a small saucepan, combine peanut butter, coconut milk, soy sauce, brown sugar, lime juice, minced garlic, and red pepper flakes.

- Heat over low heat, stirring constantly until smooth and well combined. If the sauce is too thick, gradually add water, a tablespoon at a time, until desired consistency is reached. Remove from heat and set aside.
4. **Skewer and Grill the Chicken:**
   - Preheat your grill or grill pan over medium-high heat.
   - Thread marinated chicken strips onto the soaked skewers, shaking off excess marinade.
5. **Grill the Chicken Satay:**
   - Grill the chicken satay skewers for about 3-4 minutes per side, or until cooked through and nicely charred. Cooking time may vary depending on the thickness of the chicken strips.
6. **Serve:**
   - Arrange grilled chicken satay skewers on a platter.
   - Serve with the prepared peanut sauce on the side for dipping or drizzling.
   - Garnish with chopped fresh cilantro and sliced red chili peppers, if desired.

Enjoy these flavorful and juicy chicken satay skewers with the creamy peanut sauce as a delicious appetizer or main dish. They're perfect for parties, barbecues, or any time you're craving authentic Southeast Asian flavors!

Vegetarian Paella

Ingredients:

- 1 cup Bomba or Arborio rice
- 2 cups vegetable broth
- 1 onion, diced
- 2 cloves garlic, minced
- 1 red bell pepper, sliced
- 1 yellow bell pepper, sliced
- 1 zucchini, diced
- 1 cup green beans, trimmed and halved
- 1 cup cherry tomatoes, halved
- 1 cup cooked chickpeas or white beans
- 1/2 cup frozen peas
- 1/2 teaspoon smoked paprika
- 1/2 teaspoon sweet paprika
- 1/2 teaspoon saffron threads, steeped in 1/4 cup hot water
- Salt and pepper, to taste
- Olive oil
- Lemon wedges, for serving
- Fresh parsley or cilantro, chopped, for garnish

Instructions:

1. **Prepare the saffron infusion:**
   - In a small bowl, steep the saffron threads in 1/4 cup hot water. Set aside to infuse.
2. **Sauté vegetables:**
   - Heat olive oil in a large paella pan or wide skillet over medium heat.
   - Add diced onion and sauté until translucent, about 5 minutes.
   - Add minced garlic and cook for another minute until fragrant.
   - Stir in sliced bell peppers, diced zucchini, and halved cherry tomatoes. Cook for 5-7 minutes until vegetables start to soften.
3. **Add rice and spices:**
   - Stir in Bomba or Arborio rice, smoked paprika, and sweet paprika. Cook for 1-2 minutes, stirring constantly, until rice is coated with oil and spices.
4. **Simmer with broth and saffron:**
   - Pour vegetable broth and the saffron infusion (with threads) over the rice mixture. Season with salt and pepper to taste.
   - Bring to a boil, then reduce heat to medium-low. Simmer uncovered for about 15-20 minutes, without stirring, until most of the liquid is absorbed and rice is almost tender. Add more broth if needed to keep the rice moist.
5. **Add beans and peas:**

- Nestle cooked chickpeas or white beans and frozen peas into the rice mixture. Arrange them evenly.
6. **Finish and serve:**
    - Cover the paella pan with foil or a lid and cook for another 5-10 minutes, until the rice is fully cooked and all liquid is absorbed.
    - Remove from heat and let it rest, covered, for 5-10 minutes to allow flavors to meld.
    - Garnish with chopped fresh parsley or cilantro.
    - Serve vegetarian paella hot, with lemon wedges on the side for squeezing over individual servings.

This vegetarian paella is a colorful and satisfying dish that captures the essence of Spanish cuisine with its vibrant vegetables and aromatic saffron-infused rice. Enjoy it as a main course or as part of a festive meal with friends and family!

Clam Chowder

Ingredients:

- 2 slices bacon, chopped (optional)
- 1 onion, diced
- 2 stalks celery, diced
- 2 tablespoons butter
- 3 tablespoons all-purpose flour
- 2 cups chicken broth or seafood broth
- 1 cup milk
- 1 cup heavy cream
- 3 cups potatoes, peeled and diced into small cubes
- 2 cans (6.5 oz each) chopped clams, drained, with juices reserved
- Salt and pepper, to taste
- Fresh parsley, chopped, for garnish (optional)
- Oyster crackers or crusty bread, for serving

Instructions:

1. **Cook the bacon (if using):**
   - In a large pot or Dutch oven, cook chopped bacon over medium heat until crispy. Remove bacon with a slotted spoon and set aside on a paper towel-lined plate.
2. **Sauté vegetables:**
   - In the same pot, add diced onion, celery, and butter. Sauté over medium heat until vegetables are softened, about 5-7 minutes.
3. **Make the roux:**
   - Sprinkle flour over the vegetables and stir to coat. Cook for 1-2 minutes, stirring constantly, to cook out the raw flour taste.
4. **Add liquids:**
   - Gradually whisk in chicken broth, milk, and heavy cream, stirring constantly to prevent lumps. Bring to a simmer.
5. **Add potatoes and clams:**
   - Add diced potatoes and reserved clam juice (from the cans). Simmer for about 15-20 minutes, or until potatoes are tender and cooked through.
6. **Finish the chowder:**
   - Stir in chopped clams (from the cans). Season with salt and pepper to taste.
   - If the chowder is too thick, you can add more milk or broth to achieve your desired consistency.
   - Let the chowder simmer for another 5-10 minutes to allow flavors to meld together.
7. **Serve:**
   - Ladle clam chowder into bowls. Garnish with crispy bacon (if using) and chopped fresh parsley.
   - Serve hot, accompanied by oyster crackers or crusty bread.

Enjoy this rich and creamy clam chowder, packed with tender clams, potatoes, and savory bacon flavors. It's perfect for a cozy meal on a chilly day!

Pork Schnitzel

Ingredients:

- 4 boneless pork chops, about 1/2 inch thick (you can also use pork tenderloin and slice into thin cutlets)
- Salt and pepper, to taste
- 1/2 cup all-purpose flour
- 2 large eggs, beaten
- 1 cup breadcrumbs (preferably fresh, or use Panko breadcrumbs)
- 1/2 cup grated Parmesan cheese (optional, for extra flavor)
- 1 teaspoon paprika
- Vegetable oil, for frying
- Lemon wedges, for serving
- Fresh parsley, chopped, for garnish (optional)

Instructions:

1. **Prepare the pork cutlets:**
    - Place each pork chop between two sheets of plastic wrap or parchment paper. Use a meat mallet or rolling pin to pound the pork chops until they are about 1/4 inch thick. This helps tenderize the meat and ensures even cooking.
2. **Season and dredge:**
    - Season the pounded pork cutlets with salt and pepper on both sides.
    - Set up three shallow dishes: one with flour, one with beaten eggs, and one with breadcrumbs mixed with grated Parmesan cheese (if using) and paprika.
3. **Coat the pork cutlets:**
    - Dredge each pork cutlet in the flour, shaking off any excess.
    - Dip into the beaten eggs, allowing any excess to drip off.
    - Press the pork cutlets into the breadcrumb mixture, ensuring they are evenly coated on both sides. Gently press the breadcrumbs onto the meat to help them adhere.
4. **Fry the schnitzel:**
    - In a large skillet, heat enough vegetable oil over medium-high heat to shallow fry the pork cutlets (about 1/4 inch deep).
    - Once the oil is hot (test by dropping a breadcrumb in - it should sizzle immediately), carefully place the breaded pork cutlets into the skillet in a single layer, without overcrowding. You may need to fry in batches.
    - Cook each schnitzel for 3-4 minutes on each side, or until they are golden brown and cooked through. The internal temperature of the pork should reach 145°F (63°C) for safe consumption.
    - Transfer the cooked schnitzels to a plate lined with paper towels to drain excess oil.
5. **Serve:**

- Serve pork schnitzel hot, garnished with lemon wedges for squeezing over the cutlets.
- Optionally, sprinkle with chopped fresh parsley for added freshness.

Pork schnitzel is traditionally served with lemon wedges for acidity and freshness, and it pairs well with sides like potato salad, cucumber salad, or mashed potatoes. Enjoy this crispy and delicious dish that's a favorite in German cuisine!

Gazpacho

Ingredients:

- 6 ripe tomatoes, chopped
- 1 cucumber, peeled, seeded, and chopped
- 1 red bell pepper, seeded and chopped
- 1 green bell pepper, seeded and chopped
- 1 small red onion, chopped
- 2 cloves garlic, minced
- 3 cups tomato juice
- 1/4 cup extra virgin olive oil
- 2 tablespoons red wine vinegar or sherry vinegar
- 1 tablespoon fresh lemon juice
- 1 teaspoon salt, or to taste
- 1/2 teaspoon ground black pepper
- 1/2 teaspoon ground cumin (optional)
- Dash of hot sauce (optional, for heat)
- Fresh herbs (such as parsley or cilantro), chopped, for garnish

Instructions:

1. **Prepare the vegetables:**
   - In a large bowl, combine chopped tomatoes, cucumber, red bell pepper, green bell pepper, red onion, and minced garlic.
2. **Blend the soup:**
   - Working in batches if necessary, transfer the chopped vegetables to a blender or food processor. Pulse until the mixture is mostly smooth but still slightly chunky. Add tomato juice as needed to achieve the desired consistency.
3. **Season the gazpacho:**
   - Transfer the blended mixture back to the large bowl.
   - Stir in extra virgin olive oil, red wine vinegar or sherry vinegar, fresh lemon juice, salt, pepper, and ground cumin (if using). Taste and adjust seasoning as needed. Add a dash of hot sauce if you prefer a bit of heat.
4. **Chill:**
   - Cover the gazpacho and refrigerate for at least 2 hours, or preferably overnight, to allow the flavors to meld and develop.
5. **Serve:**
   - Stir the gazpacho well before serving.
   - Ladle chilled gazpacho into bowls.
   - Garnish with chopped fresh herbs, such as parsley or cilantro.
   - Optionally, drizzle with a little extra virgin olive oil before serving.

Gazpacho is typically served cold and can be enjoyed as a refreshing appetizer or light meal. Serve with crusty bread or croutons for added texture. It's a healthy and flavorful dish that celebrates the vibrant flavors of fresh vegetables!

Chicken Marsala

Ingredients:

- 4 boneless, skinless chicken breasts
- Salt and pepper, to taste
- 1/2 cup all-purpose flour, for dredging
- 4 tablespoons unsalted butter, divided
- 2 tablespoons olive oil
- 8 oz (225g) mushrooms, sliced
- 1/2 cup Marsala wine
- 1/2 cup chicken broth
- 1/2 cup heavy cream (optional, for a creamier sauce)
- Fresh parsley, chopped, for garnish

Instructions:

1. **Prepare the chicken:**
    - Place each chicken breast between two sheets of plastic wrap or parchment paper. Use a meat mallet or rolling pin to pound the chicken to an even thickness of about 1/4 inch. Season both sides with salt and pepper.
2. **Dredge the chicken:**
    - Dredge the chicken breasts in flour, shaking off any excess.
3. **Cook the chicken:**
    - In a large skillet, heat 2 tablespoons of butter and 2 tablespoons of olive oil over medium-high heat.
    - Add the chicken breasts to the skillet and cook for about 3-4 minutes per side, or until golden brown and cooked through. Remove chicken from skillet and set aside on a plate.
4. **Make the Marsala sauce:**
    - In the same skillet, melt the remaining 2 tablespoons of butter. Add sliced mushrooms and sauté until they are golden brown and the liquid has evaporated, about 5-7 minutes.
5. **Deglaze the skillet:**
    - Pour Marsala wine into the skillet, scraping up any browned bits from the bottom of the pan. Let the wine simmer for a few minutes until it reduces slightly.
6. **Add broth and cream:**
    - Stir in chicken broth and bring to a simmer. If using heavy cream for a creamier sauce, add it now and stir well.
7. **Simmer and finish:**
    - Return the chicken breasts to the skillet and simmer in the sauce for another 5-7 minutes, or until the chicken is heated through and the sauce has thickened slightly.
8. **Serve:**
    - Garnish Chicken Marsala with chopped fresh parsley.

- Serve hot, with the Marsala sauce spooned over the chicken breasts.

Chicken Marsala pairs beautifully with pasta, rice, or mashed potatoes, making it a versatile and comforting dish that's perfect for a special dinner or entertaining guests. Enjoy the rich flavors of this classic Italian dish!

Spinach and Ricotta Stuffed Shells

Ingredients:

- 1 box (12 oz) jumbo pasta shells
- 1 tablespoon olive oil
- 3 cloves garlic, minced
- 1 (10 oz) package frozen chopped spinach, thawed and squeezed dry
- 15 oz ricotta cheese
- 1 cup shredded mozzarella cheese, divided
- 1/2 cup grated Parmesan cheese, divided
- 1 egg, lightly beaten
- 1 teaspoon dried oregano
- 1/2 teaspoon dried basil
- Salt and pepper, to taste
- 2 cups marinara sauce

Instructions:

1. **Cook the pasta shells:**
    - Bring a large pot of salted water to a boil. Cook the jumbo pasta shells according to package instructions until al dente. Drain and rinse under cold water to stop the cooking process. Set aside.
2. **Prepare the filling:**
    - In a large skillet, heat olive oil over medium heat. Add minced garlic and sauté for 1-2 minutes until fragrant.
    - Add thawed and squeezed dry spinach to the skillet. Cook for another 2-3 minutes, stirring occasionally, until any excess moisture has evaporated. Remove from heat and let it cool slightly.
3. **Make the ricotta mixture:**
    - In a large mixing bowl, combine ricotta cheese, 3/4 cup shredded mozzarella cheese, 1/4 cup grated Parmesan cheese, beaten egg, dried oregano, dried basil, salt, and pepper.
    - Add the cooked spinach and garlic mixture to the ricotta mixture. Stir until well combined.
4. **Stuff the pasta shells:**
    - Preheat your oven to 350°F (175°C). Spread a thin layer of marinara sauce on the bottom of a 9x13-inch baking dish.
    - Using a spoon, fill each cooked pasta shell with the spinach and ricotta mixture, packing it tightly. Place the stuffed shells in the prepared baking dish.
5. **Bake:**
    - Pour the remaining marinara sauce evenly over the stuffed shells in the baking dish.
    - Sprinkle the remaining 1/4 cup shredded mozzarella cheese and 1/4 cup grated Parmesan cheese over the top.

- Cover the baking dish with aluminum foil and bake in the preheated oven for 25-30 minutes, or until the cheese is melted and bubbly.
6. **Serve:**
    - Remove from the oven and let it cool for a few minutes before serving.
    - Garnish with fresh basil or parsley if desired.
    - Serve warm and enjoy these delicious spinach and ricotta stuffed shells as a satisfying main dish!

This dish is sure to please with its creamy spinach and ricotta filling, paired perfectly with marinara sauce and melted cheese. It's a comforting and crowd-pleasing meal that's great for family dinners or gatherings!

Tuna Nicoise Salad

Ingredients:

For the Salad:

- 1 lb (450g) baby potatoes, halved or quartered
- 8 oz (225g) green beans, trimmed
- 4 large eggs
- 1 lb (450g) fresh tuna steak, about 1 inch thick
- Salt and pepper, to taste
- 1 tablespoon olive oil
- 4 cups mixed salad greens (such as arugula, spinach, or lettuce)
- 1 cup cherry tomatoes, halved
- 1/2 cup Nicoise olives (or Kalamata olives)
- 2 tablespoons capers (optional)

For the Vinaigrette:

- 1/4 cup extra virgin olive oil
- 2 tablespoons red wine vinegar
- 1 tablespoon Dijon mustard
- 1 clove garlic, minced
- 1 teaspoon honey (optional, for sweetness)
- Salt and pepper, to taste

Instructions:

1. **Prepare the vegetables:**
   - In a medium pot, bring salted water to a boil. Add halved baby potatoes and cook until tender, about 10-12 minutes. Drain and set aside.
   - In the same pot of boiling water (or another pot), blanch green beans for 3-4 minutes until crisp-tender. Drain and immediately plunge into ice water to stop cooking. Drain again and set aside.
2. **Hard-boil the eggs:**
   - Place eggs in a small saucepan and cover with cold water. Bring to a boil over medium-high heat. Once boiling, cover, remove from heat, and let stand for 9-10 minutes.
   - Transfer eggs to a bowl of ice water to cool. Once cooled, peel and quarter the eggs.
3. **Cook the tuna:**
   - Pat dry the tuna steak with paper towels. Season with salt and pepper.
   - In a large skillet or grill pan, heat olive oil over medium-high heat. Cook the tuna steak for about 2-3 minutes per side, or until desired doneness (medium-rare is

recommended for best flavor). Remove from heat and let it rest for a few minutes before slicing.
4. **Make the vinaigrette:**
   - In a small bowl, whisk together extra virgin olive oil, red wine vinegar, Dijon mustard, minced garlic, honey (if using), salt, and pepper until well combined.
5. **Assemble the salad:**
   - Arrange mixed salad greens on a large serving platter or individual plates.
   - Arrange cooked baby potatoes, blanched green beans, cherry tomatoes, Nicoise olives, and capers (if using) over the greens.
   - Slice the cooked tuna steak and place on top of the salad.
   - Arrange quartered hard-boiled eggs around the salad.
6. **Serve:**
   - Drizzle the vinaigrette over the Tuna Nicoise Salad just before serving.
   - Garnish with additional fresh herbs, such as parsley or basil, if desired.

Tuna Nicoise Salad is a complete meal in itself, packed with protein and fresh vegetables. It's a perfect choice for a light lunch or dinner, especially during warmer months when you crave something refreshing and satisfying. Enjoy the flavors and textures of this classic French salad!

Bangers and Mash

Ingredients:

For the Bangers:

- 8 pork sausages (traditionally Cumberland or Lincolnshire sausages)
- 1 tablespoon vegetable oil

For the Mashed Potatoes:

- 2 lbs (about 1 kg) potatoes, peeled and cut into chunks
- Salt, to taste
- 4 tablespoons butter
- 1/2 cup milk, warmed
- Freshly ground black pepper, to taste

For the Onion Gravy:

- 2 onions, thinly sliced
- 2 tablespoons butter
- 2 tablespoons all-purpose flour
- 2 cups beef or chicken broth
- 1 tablespoon Worcestershire sauce
- Salt and pepper, to taste

Instructions:

1. **Cook the Sausages (Bangers):**
    - Heat vegetable oil in a large skillet over medium-high heat. Add the sausages and cook, turning occasionally, until browned and cooked through, about 10-12 minutes. Reduce heat if they brown too quickly. Once cooked, transfer to a plate and cover to keep warm.
2. **Make the Mashed Potatoes:**
    - While the sausages are cooking, place peeled and chopped potatoes in a large pot and cover with cold water. Add a generous pinch of salt.
    - Bring to a boil over medium-high heat, then reduce heat to medium-low and simmer until potatoes are tender when pierced with a fork, about 15-20 minutes.
    - Drain the potatoes well and return them to the pot. Add butter and warm milk. Mash the potatoes until smooth and creamy. Season with salt and pepper to taste. Keep warm.
3. **Prepare the Onion Gravy:**
    - In the same skillet used for cooking sausages, melt butter over medium heat. Add sliced onions and cook until softened and caramelized, about 10-15 minutes.
    - Sprinkle flour over the onions and stir well to combine, cooking for 1-2 minutes to cook out the raw flour taste.

- Gradually whisk in beef or chicken broth, scraping up any browned bits from the bottom of the skillet. Bring to a simmer and cook until the gravy thickens, stirring occasionally, about 5-7 minutes.
- Stir in Worcestershire sauce and season with salt and pepper to taste.

4. **Assemble and Serve:**
    - To serve, place a generous spoonful of mashed potatoes on each plate.
    - Arrange cooked sausages on top of the mashed potatoes.
    - Pour onion gravy over the sausages and mashed potatoes.
    - Garnish with chopped fresh parsley or thyme, if desired.

Bangers and mash is a comforting and satisfying dish, perfect for a cozy dinner. It's a classic British pub favorite that pairs well with a pint of beer or a glass of cider. Enjoy the hearty flavors of this traditional dish!

Lemon Garlic Roast Chicken

Ingredients:

- 1 whole chicken (about 4-5 lbs or 1.8-2.3 kg), giblets removed
- 2 lemons, divided
- 6 cloves garlic, minced
- 2 tablespoons olive oil
- 2 tablespoons melted butter
- 1 teaspoon dried thyme (or 1 tablespoon fresh thyme leaves)
- 1 teaspoon dried rosemary (or 1 tablespoon fresh rosemary leaves), chopped
- Salt and pepper, to taste
- Fresh parsley, chopped, for garnish (optional)

Instructions:

1. **Prepare the chicken:**
    - Preheat your oven to 400°F (200°C).
    - Rinse the chicken under cold water and pat dry with paper towels. Place the chicken in a roasting pan or baking dish.
2. **Prepare the lemon garlic mixture:**
    - Zest one of the lemons and juice both lemons. In a small bowl, combine the lemon zest, lemon juice, minced garlic, olive oil, melted butter, dried thyme, dried rosemary, salt, and pepper. Mix well to combine.
3. **Season the chicken:**
    - Carefully lift the skin of the chicken and rub half of the lemon garlic mixture underneath the skin, spreading it evenly over the breast and thighs.
    - Rub the remaining lemon garlic mixture all over the outside of the chicken, ensuring it's coated evenly. Season the chicken generously with salt and pepper.
4. **Roast the chicken:**
    - Place the chicken in the preheated oven and roast for about 1 hour and 15 minutes to 1 hour and 30 minutes, or until the internal temperature reaches 165°F (75°C) when measured with a meat thermometer inserted into the thickest part of the thigh without touching bone.
5. **Rest and serve:**
    - Once the chicken is cooked through, remove it from the oven and let it rest for 10-15 minutes before carving.
    - Garnish with chopped fresh parsley, if desired, before serving.
6. **Serve:**
    - Carve the lemon garlic roast chicken into pieces and serve hot. You can serve it with roasted vegetables, mashed potatoes, or a fresh salad on the side.

This lemon garlic roast chicken is tender, juicy, and infused with citrus and herb flavors. It makes for a comforting and satisfying meal that's perfect for any occasion, from casual family dinners to special gatherings. Enjoy the deliciousness of homemade roast chicken!

Beef Kefta

Ingredients:

- 1 lb (450g) ground beef (preferably lean)
- 1 small onion, grated or finely minced
- 2 cloves garlic, minced
- 1/4 cup fresh parsley, finely chopped
- 1/4 cup fresh cilantro, finely chopped
- 1 teaspoon ground cumin
- 1 teaspoon ground coriander
- 1/2 teaspoon paprika
- 1/2 teaspoon ground cinnamon
- 1/4 teaspoon cayenne pepper (optional, for heat)
- Salt and pepper, to taste
- 2 tablespoons olive oil, for grilling or pan-frying
- Lemon wedges, for serving

Instructions:

1. **Prepare the kefta mixture:**
   - In a large mixing bowl, combine ground beef, grated or minced onion, minced garlic, chopped parsley, chopped cilantro, ground cumin, ground coriander, paprika, ground cinnamon, cayenne pepper (if using), salt, and pepper. Mix well until all ingredients are evenly distributed.
2. **Shape the kefta:**
   - Take a portion of the beef mixture and shape it into elongated patties or cylinder shapes, about 2 inches long and 1 inch thick. You can also skewer the kefta mixture onto metal or soaked wooden skewers.
3. **Cook the kefta:**
   - Heat olive oil in a large skillet or grill pan over medium-high heat. Alternatively, you can grill the kefta on an outdoor grill over medium heat.
   - Cook the kefta for about 4-5 minutes per side, or until browned and cooked through. Ensure the internal temperature reaches 160°F (71°C) for safe consumption.
4. **Serve:**
   - Transfer the cooked beef kefta to a serving platter. Serve hot with lemon wedges on the side for squeezing over the kefta.
   - Optional: Serve with pita bread, rice, or couscous, and a side of tzatziki or tahini sauce for dipping.

Beef kefta is flavorful and aromatic, with the combination of herbs and spices giving it a delicious depth of flavor. It's a versatile dish that can be enjoyed as an appetizer, main course, or part of a mezze platter. Enjoy the rich taste of homemade beef kefta with this simple and authentic recipe!

Egg Drop Soup

Ingredients:

- 4 cups chicken broth (homemade or store-bought)
- 2 tablespoons cornstarch
- 2 tablespoons water
- 2 eggs
- 1 teaspoon soy sauce
- 1/2 teaspoon sesame oil
- Salt and white pepper, to taste
- 2 green onions, thinly sliced (optional, for garnish)

Instructions:

1. **Prepare the broth:**
   - In a medium pot, bring the chicken broth to a simmer over medium heat.
2. **Thicken the soup (optional step):**
   - In a small bowl, mix cornstarch with water to create a slurry. Stir until smooth.
   - Gradually pour the cornstarch slurry into the simmering broth, stirring constantly. Cook for 1-2 minutes, or until the broth slightly thickens. This step is optional and can be skipped if you prefer a lighter consistency.
3. **Beat the eggs:**
   - In a separate bowl, beat the eggs together with soy sauce and sesame oil until well combined.
4. **Add the eggs to the soup:**
   - Once the broth is simmering, use a fork or chopsticks to stir the broth in a circular motion. Slowly pour the beaten eggs into the swirling broth. The eggs will cook immediately and form thin ribbons.
5. **Season and serve:**
   - Season the soup with salt and white pepper, adjusting to taste.
   - Remove the pot from heat. Ladle the egg drop soup into bowls.
   - Garnish with thinly sliced green onions, if desired.
6. **Serve hot:**
   - Serve the egg drop soup immediately while hot, as it's best enjoyed fresh.

Egg drop soup is light, soothing, and perfect as a starter or light meal. It's a quick and easy dish to make at home, showcasing the delicate flavor of eggs in a savory broth. Customize it with additional ingredients like tofu, mushrooms, or bamboo shoots for added texture and flavor. Enjoy this comforting Chinese classic!

Swedish Meatballs

Ingredients:

For the Meatballs:

- 1 lb (450g) ground beef (or a mix of ground beef and pork)
- 1/2 cup breadcrumbs
- 1/4 cup milk
- 1 small onion, finely chopped or grated
- 1 garlic clove, minced
- 1 egg
- 1/2 teaspoon salt
- 1/4 teaspoon black pepper
- 1/4 teaspoon ground allspice
- 1/4 teaspoon ground nutmeg
- 1/4 teaspoon ground cardamom (optional)
- 2 tablespoons butter or oil, for frying

For the Gravy:

- 2 tablespoons butter
- 2 tablespoons all-purpose flour
- 2 cups beef broth
- 1/2 cup heavy cream
- 1 tablespoon soy sauce (optional, for extra flavor)
- Salt and pepper, to taste
- Fresh parsley, chopped, for garnish (optional)

Instructions:

1. **Make the Meatballs:**
    - In a small bowl, combine breadcrumbs and milk. Let it sit for a few minutes until the breadcrumbs absorb the milk.
    - In a large mixing bowl, combine ground beef, soaked breadcrumbs, finely chopped onion, minced garlic, egg, salt, pepper, allspice, nutmeg, and cardamom (if using). Mix until well combined.
    - Shape the mixture into small meatballs, about 1 inch in diameter.
2. **Cook the Meatballs:**
    - In a large skillet, heat 2 tablespoons of butter or oil over medium-high heat.
    - Add the meatballs in batches, being careful not to overcrowd the pan. Cook for about 4-5 minutes, turning occasionally, until browned on all sides and cooked through. Transfer cooked meatballs to a plate and cover to keep warm.
3. **Make the Gravy:**

- In the same skillet used for cooking the meatballs, melt 2 tablespoons of butter over medium heat.
- Sprinkle flour over the melted butter and whisk continuously to form a roux. Cook for 1-2 minutes until lightly golden brown.
- Gradually whisk in beef broth, scraping up any browned bits from the bottom of the skillet. Bring to a simmer and cook for 2-3 minutes, stirring occasionally, until the gravy thickens slightly.

4. **Finish the Dish:**
    - Stir in heavy cream and soy sauce (if using). Season with salt and pepper to taste.
    - Return the meatballs to the skillet, coating them with the gravy. Simmer gently for another 2-3 minutes to heat through.

5. **Serve:**
    - Transfer Swedish meatballs and gravy to a serving dish.
    - Garnish with chopped fresh parsley, if desired.
    - Serve hot, traditionally over mashed potatoes or egg noodles.

Swedish meatballs are rich, flavorful, and perfect for a comforting meal. The combination of spices and creamy gravy makes them a favorite for family dinners or special occasions. Enjoy the homemade goodness of Swedish meatballs with this delicious recipe!

Pesto Pasta

Ingredients:

- 12 oz (340g) pasta of your choice (such as spaghetti, linguine, or penne)
- 2 cups fresh basil leaves, packed
- 1/2 cup grated Parmesan cheese
- 1/2 cup pine nuts or walnuts
- 2 garlic cloves, peeled
- 1/2 cup extra virgin olive oil
- Salt and freshly ground black pepper, to taste
- Optional: Cherry tomatoes, halved, and extra Parmesan cheese for garnish

Instructions:

1. **Cook the pasta:**
    - Bring a large pot of salted water to a boil. Cook the pasta according to package instructions until al dente. Reserve about 1/2 cup of pasta cooking water, then drain the pasta.
2. **Make the pesto:**
    - In a food processor, combine basil leaves, grated Parmesan cheese, pine nuts or walnuts, and garlic cloves. Pulse until coarsely chopped.
    - With the food processor running, gradually add the olive oil in a steady stream until the pesto is smooth and well combined. Scrape down the sides of the processor bowl as needed.
    - Season with salt and pepper to taste. If the pesto is too thick, you can add a little more olive oil or some of the reserved pasta cooking water to thin it out.
3. **Combine pasta and pesto:**
    - In a large serving bowl, toss the cooked pasta with the freshly made pesto until well coated. If desired, add a splash of the reserved pasta cooking water to help the pesto evenly coat the pasta.
4. **Serve:**
    - Garnish the pesto pasta with halved cherry tomatoes and extra grated Parmesan cheese, if desired.
    - Serve immediately, as pesto pasta is best enjoyed fresh and warm.

Pesto pasta is a quick and satisfying dish that can be enjoyed on its own or paired with grilled chicken, shrimp, or roasted vegetables for added protein and texture. It's a versatile and delicious meal that's perfect for both weeknight dinners and special occasions. Enjoy the fresh and aromatic flavors of homemade pesto pasta!

Chicken Caesar Wraps

Ingredients:

- 2 boneless, skinless chicken breasts
- Salt and pepper, to taste
- 1 tablespoon olive oil
- 4 large flour tortillas or wraps
- 2 cups romaine lettuce, chopped
- 1/2 cup grated Parmesan cheese
- Caesar dressing (store-bought or homemade, see below)
- Optional additions: cherry tomatoes (halved), croutons, avocado slices

For Caesar Dressing (if making from scratch):

- 1/2 cup mayonnaise
- 2 tablespoons grated Parmesan cheese
- 1 tablespoon lemon juice
- 1 teaspoon Dijon mustard
- 1 garlic clove, minced
- Salt and pepper, to taste

Instructions:

1. **Cook the chicken:**
   - Season chicken breasts with salt and pepper on both sides.
   - In a large skillet, heat olive oil over medium-high heat. Cook chicken breasts for about 6-7 minutes per side, or until fully cooked (internal temperature should reach 165°F or 74°C). Remove from heat and let them rest for a few minutes. Slice or shred the chicken into thin strips.
2. **Make the Caesar dressing (if making from scratch):**
   - In a small bowl, whisk together mayonnaise, grated Parmesan cheese, lemon juice, Dijon mustard, minced garlic, salt, and pepper until smooth and well combined. Adjust seasoning to taste.
3. **Assemble the wraps:**
   - Lay out the flour tortillas or wraps on a clean surface.
   - Spread a generous amount of Caesar dressing onto each tortilla.
   - Divide chopped romaine lettuce evenly among the tortillas.
   - Top with sliced or shredded cooked chicken, grated Parmesan cheese, and any optional additions such as cherry tomatoes, croutons, or avocado slices.
4. **Wrap and serve:**
   - Fold in the sides of each tortilla, then roll tightly from the bottom up to enclose the filling.
   - Cut each wrap in half diagonally, if desired, and serve immediately.

Chicken Caesar wraps are a delicious lunch or light dinner option that's packed with protein and fresh flavors. They're easy to customize based on personal preferences and can be prepared ahead of time for a quick grab-and-go meal. Enjoy the classic combination of chicken, Caesar dressing, and crisp romaine lettuce in these satisfying wraps!

Moroccan Tagine

Ingredients:

- 1 lb (450g) boneless, skinless chicken thighs, cut into bite-sized pieces (or lamb, beef, or vegetables for vegetarian option)
- 2 tablespoons olive oil
- 1 large onion, finely chopped
- 3 cloves garlic, minced
- 1 tablespoon grated fresh ginger
- 1 teaspoon ground cumin
- 1 teaspoon ground coriander
- 1 teaspoon ground turmeric
- 1/2 teaspoon ground cinnamon
- 1/4 teaspoon ground cloves
- 1/4 teaspoon ground nutmeg
- Pinch of saffron threads (optional, for added flavor)
- 1 can (14 oz or 400g) diced tomatoes, with juices
- 1 cup chicken broth (or vegetable broth for vegetarian option)
- 1 cup dried apricots, halved (or raisins)
- 1/2 cup green olives, pitted
- Salt and pepper, to taste
- Fresh cilantro or parsley, chopped, for garnish
- Cooked couscous or rice, for serving

Instructions:

1. **Prepare the chicken (or meat/vegetables):**
    - Heat olive oil in a large skillet or tagine over medium-high heat. Add the chicken pieces and cook until browned on all sides. Remove from the skillet and set aside.
2. **Cook the aromatics:**
    - In the same skillet or tagine, add chopped onion and cook until softened and translucent, about 5 minutes.
    - Add minced garlic and grated ginger, and cook for another 1-2 minutes until fragrant.
3. **Add spices and liquids:**
    - Stir in ground cumin, ground coriander, ground turmeric, ground cinnamon, ground cloves, ground nutmeg, and saffron threads (if using). Cook for 1 minute until spices are fragrant.
    - Pour in diced tomatoes with their juices and chicken broth. Stir to combine, scraping up any browned bits from the bottom of the skillet.
4. **Simmer the tagine:**
    - Return the browned chicken pieces to the skillet/tagine. Bring the mixture to a simmer.

- Reduce heat to low, cover, and let simmer gently for 30-40 minutes, stirring occasionally, until the chicken is tender and cooked through. If using lamb or beef, cooking time may need to be adjusted for tenderness.
5. **Add dried fruits and olives:**
    - Stir in dried apricots (or raisins) and green olives. Simmer for an additional 10 minutes, allowing flavors to meld together.
    - Season with salt and pepper to taste.
6. **Serve:**
    - Garnish Moroccan tagine with chopped fresh cilantro or parsley.
    - Serve hot over cooked couscous or rice.

Moroccan tagine is known for its rich flavors and the combination of sweet and savory elements from the dried fruits, spices, and tender meat. It's a comforting and satisfying dish that's perfect for sharing with family and friends. Enjoy the exotic tastes of Moroccan cuisine with this hearty tagine recipe!

Ratatouille

Ingredients:

- 1 large eggplant, diced
- 2 medium zucchinis, diced
- 1 red bell pepper, diced
- 1 yellow bell pepper, diced
- 1 onion, finely chopped
- 3 cloves garlic, minced
- 4 tomatoes, diced (or 1 can (14 oz) diced tomatoes)
- 2 tablespoons tomato paste
- 1/4 cup olive oil
- 1 teaspoon dried thyme (or 1 tablespoon fresh thyme leaves)
- 1 teaspoon dried oregano
- Salt and pepper, to taste
- Fresh basil leaves, chopped, for garnish (optional)

Instructions:

1. **Prepare the vegetables:**
   - Dice the eggplant, zucchinis, red bell pepper, yellow bell pepper, and tomatoes into evenly sized pieces.
2. **Cook the onion and garlic:**
   - In a large skillet or Dutch oven, heat olive oil over medium heat. Add chopped onion and cook until softened and translucent, about 5 minutes.
   - Add minced garlic and cook for another 1-2 minutes until fragrant.
3. **Cook the vegetables:**
   - Add diced eggplant to the skillet and cook for 5-7 minutes, stirring occasionally, until softened.
   - Stir in diced zucchinis, red bell pepper, and yellow bell pepper. Cook for an additional 5 minutes, until vegetables are slightly tender.
4. **Add tomatoes and seasonings:**
   - Stir in diced tomatoes (or canned diced tomatoes with their juices) and tomato paste. Mix well to combine.
   - Season with dried thyme, dried oregano, salt, and pepper. Stir to distribute the seasonings evenly.
5. **Simmer the ratatouille:**
   - Reduce heat to low and cover the skillet or Dutch oven. Let the ratatouille simmer gently for 20-30 minutes, stirring occasionally, until all vegetables are tender and flavors have melded together.
6. **Serve:**
   - Remove from heat and let the ratatouille rest for a few minutes before serving.
   - Garnish with chopped fresh basil leaves, if desired.

- Serve hot or at room temperature as a side dish, over rice or pasta, or as a main dish with crusty bread.

Ratatouille is a versatile dish that can be enjoyed warm or cold, and it's perfect for using up an abundance of summer vegetables. Its rustic flavors and vibrant colors make it a delightful addition to any meal. Enjoy the taste of Provence with this homemade ratatouille recipe!

Chocolate Lava Cakes

Ingredients:

- 1/2 cup (1 stick) unsalted butter, plus extra for greasing ramekins
- 4 oz (113g) semi-sweet or bittersweet chocolate, chopped
- 2 large eggs
- 2 large egg yolks
- 1/4 cup granulated sugar
- 1 teaspoon vanilla extract
- 2 tablespoons all-purpose flour
- Pinch of salt
- Powdered sugar, for dusting (optional)
- Vanilla ice cream or whipped cream, for serving (optional)

Instructions:

1. **Prepare the ramekins:**
   - Preheat your oven to 425°F (220°C). Grease four 6-ounce ramekins with butter and dust lightly with cocoa powder or flour, shaking out any excess. Place the ramekins on a baking sheet.
2. **Melt the butter and chocolate:**
   - In a medium microwave-safe bowl, melt the butter and chopped chocolate together in the microwave in 30-second intervals, stirring well after each interval, until smooth and fully melted. Alternatively, melt over a double boiler on the stove, stirring constantly.
3. **Mix the batter:**
   - In a large bowl, whisk together eggs, egg yolks, granulated sugar, and vanilla extract until well combined.
   - Gradually pour the melted chocolate mixture into the egg mixture, whisking constantly until smooth and glossy.
4. **Add flour and salt:**
   - Sift in all-purpose flour and a pinch of salt into the chocolate mixture. Gently fold the dry ingredients into the wet mixture until just combined and no streaks of flour remain.
5. **Fill the ramekins:**
   - Divide the batter evenly among the prepared ramekins, filling each about 3/4 full.
6. **Bake the lava cakes:**
   - Place the baking sheet with the ramekins in the preheated oven. Bake for 12-14 minutes, or until the edges are set but the center still looks soft and jiggly.
7. **Serve:**
   - Carefully remove the ramekins from the oven and let them cool for 1-2 minutes.
   - Run a knife around the edges of each ramekin to loosen the cakes.
   - Invert each lava cake onto a serving plate. Dust with powdered sugar, if desired.

- - Serve immediately while warm, with a scoop of vanilla ice cream or a dollop of whipped cream on the side.

Chocolate lava cakes are best enjoyed fresh out of the oven when the center is still molten. They are a perfect treat for special occasions or when you're craving a rich, chocolatey dessert. Indulge in the irresistible combination of warm, gooey chocolate with this homemade lava cake recipe!

www.ingramcontent.com/pod-product-compliance
Lightning Source LLC
LaVergne TN
LVHW061944070526
838199LV00060B/3973